DOWN THE

A MODERN DAY

MISSISSIPPI

H U C K

NEAL**MOORE**

ON AMERICA'S RIVER ROAD

CINDY**LOVELL**

**MARK TWAIN
MUSEUM PRESS**

Mark Twain Museum Press
120 North Main Street, Hannibal, Missouri 63401

Photo credits: All chapter frontispiece photos courtesy Neal Moore
except: "Make it Right NOLA" frontispiece photo courtesy Adam Elliott.

Neal Moore and Cindy Lovell assert the moral right
to be identified as the authors of this work.

ISBN 978-0-9837169-2-1

First Edition
Printed in the United States of America

Book cover and interior design by Zarina Rose Lagman

Canoeist logo and Mississippi River map by Arron Hsueh, DDG

Down the Mississippi is available for special promotions,
including educational group discounts.

For additional photographs and video of the stories featured in
this book please visit: moderndayhuck.com

To our brothers, Tom and Allen,

who live on in our hearts, our stories, our adventures,

and who will ever be our big brothers.

—N.M. & C.L.

DOWN THE

A MODERN DAY

MISSISSIPPI

HUCK

NEAL**MOORE**

ON AMERICA'S RIVER ROAD

CINDY**LOVELL**

TABLE OF CONTENTS

PREFACE

KATHY ELDON

Whoever heard of a safari on the Mississippi River? Certainly not me – that is, until I received a call from Neal Moore, who shared his idea for a solo trip by canoe down America's mightiest river.

I had always loved hearing from Neal, ever since he telephoned to tell me that the journals of my son, Dan, had inspired him to view his life as a grand safari – an adventurous journey into the unknown. Neal told me that he had been introduced to Dan's philosophy through *The Journey is the Destination: The Journals of Dan Eldon*, a collection of Dan's journal pages that vividly recorded his trips to more than 40 countries. Neal explained that he admired Dan's adventurous spirit. But most of all he was inspired by his work as a "creative activist," using art and photography to create awareness of important issues. Tragically, Dan was killed in 1993 by a mob in Somalia, where he was working as a photojournalist for Reuters news agency. He was 22.

After Dan's death, my daughter, Amy, and I launched Creative Visions Foundation to support "creative activists" who use media and the arts to tell important stories. Over the years, extraordinary writers, photographers, filmmakers, even leaders of social movements and entrepreneurs, have contacted us to share stories about how Dan's spirit had inspired them to take on new challenges, often stretching them beyond their wildest dreams.

Jason Russell, founder of Invisible Children and director of *Kony 2012,* a film that became a viral sensation on the Internet, and Blake Mycowskie, founder of TOMS Shoes, were two amazing people who credited Dan as the spark that triggered their creative activism. But as a former journalist, I was most touched by Neal Moore, who told me how reading *The Journey is the Destination* had triggered his desire to become a citizen journalist for CNN.

However, when I heard that he was planning to canoe alone down the biggest, meanest river in America, from its headwaters in northern Minnesota to New Orleans, armed with nothing more than cameras and paddles, I must confess that I was worried. I shared with Neal concerns about his safety, but after grilling him about his plans, I realized he was more than ready to live his dream, no matter what. I felt as though I were channeling Dan when I told him: "Go for it."

After Neal set off on his watery safari, I wondered whether he would become lonely on the long journey south. However, his magnetic personality meant he attracted a seemingly endless stream of diverse and intriguing characters, all of whom would have delighted his "guiding spirit," Mark Twain. The resulting stories were entertaining, enlightening and sometimes troubling as Neal explored the challenges faced by riverside communities trying to survive in a difficult economic environment.

Neal's extraordinary book reveals his talent as a thoughtful interviewer and compelling writer, but also his commitment to living Dan's philosophy, "Safari as a way of life," which Dan described like this in his journals:

Free at last Voyages
The Search for clean water in a swamp
Energy, sincerity, clarity of vision, creativity
Mission Statement for Safari as a Way of Life
To explore the unknown and familiar, distant and near, and to record
in detail, with the eyes of a child, any beauty (of the flesh or otherwise)
horror, irony, traces of Utopia or Hell...

In reading *Down the Mississippi*, we are reminded not to forget to live our dreams, whether on adventures in faraway lands, or simply seeing things differently in our neighborhood. In our quest to live fully, there will inevitably be traces of hell along the way – Utopia, too, we hope. But the true joy of life comes when we seek to achieve our highest potential, not only for ourselves, but also for others. And in that Neal Moore has certainly succeeded.

—Kathy Eldon, Malibu, Calif., March 31, 2012

INTRODUCTION

JAMES R. PEIPERT

" *[T]he great Mississippi, the majestic, the magnificent Mississippi, rolling its mile-long tide along, shining in the sun …"*

—*Mark Twain, Life on the Mississippi,* 1883, Chapter 4

AS ONE WHO RESIDED beside the Mississippi from birth into early adulthood, I was a daily witness to the majesty and magnificence of Mark Twain's river.

As a boy, I played on the limestone bluffs that rise above the Mississippi just upriver from St Louis.

As I looked out at the river's inexorable flow, I wondered

where all that water was headed, and I fantasized about rafting down the river like Huck and Jim.

As I lay in bed at night, I listened for the mournful horns of the towboats as their pilots navigated the channel through fog, rain or snow.

As a raw youth of 17, about to graduate from a Catholic high school named for an explorer of the Mississippi, Father Jacques Marquette, I imagined the river as a magic carpet that could transport me far away from my hometown of Alton, Ill.

As I gazed at the river day after day from that high school on a hill overlooking the Mississippi, I daydreamed about finagling a job as a deckhand on one of those towboats that ply the "strong brown god," as St. Louis native T.S. Eliot called it. I could make my way to such exotic places as Memphis and New Orleans. In New Orleans, I figured, I'd sign on to a freighter bound for the ports of the seven seas.

"Moon River," a Johnny Mercer/Henry Mancini song from the 1961 film *Breakfast at Tiffany's* which speaks of two drifters off to see the world, captured my aspirations at the time. And it rattled around in my head throughout the summer of 1962, when a Marquette High School classmate and I flew to London on a Southern Illinois University charter flight and traveled throughout Europe on Mobylette mopeds bought in Brussels.

I did get to see a chunk of the world since that magical summer, mostly as a foreign correspondent for The Associated Press for 16 years. I worked in AP bureaus in

Moscow, London, Johannesburg and finally Nairobi, Kenya, where I met Kathy Eldon and her son, Dan, whose too-short life was an inspiration and impetus for the trip chronicled in this book.

More recently, I got to travel a long stretch of the Mississippi in the summer of 1996, when I rode a bicycle 740 miles from Minneapolis to St. Louis, tracking the Great River Road.

It was another bicycle ride, however, that precipitated my friendship with Neal Moore, author of this account of a journey down the Mississippi by canoe.

In 2009, as I was preparing for a bike trip across the United States from San Diego to St. Augustine, Fla., my oldest son, Ben, who teaches English in Taiwan, told me of Neal, a fellow teacher who was planning to paddle a canoe from the Mississippi's headwaters at Lake Itasca in northern Minnesota all the way down to New Orleans.

Two splendid adventures, two unlikely dreams, coming to fruition at about the same time!

A line from Henry David Thoreau's *Walden* has stuck with me since high school: "The mass of men lead lives of quiet desperation."

Thoreau may have overstated the condition of his fellow New Englanders in his musings about a sojourn in a one-room cabin at Walden Pond in Massachusetts from 1845 to 1847.

But it is probably true that relatively few people get to live their dreams, especially if the dream is, in the view of some, a bit eccentric, bizarre or just plain crazy.

For some, the chance may come late in life, as with my post-retirement bicycle ride across the United States. For others, it comes earlier, as was the case with Neal.

In a succession of emails, Neal told me of his plans to canoe the length of the Mississippi – a journey that he estimated would take about 150 days, from early July to late November or early December of 2009.

My own childhood fantasies about making my way down the river by raft or towboat never materialized. And as I grew older, I came to understand how dangerous the river can be, especially for a traveler in a small craft.

Jonathan Raban, an Englishman who journeyed down the Mississippi in 1980, described some of the dangers in a wonderful book called *Old Glory: An American Voyage.* I suggested to Neal that he read that book before he set out, thinking – maybe hoping – that he might reconsider.

Even in an aluminum 16-foot motorized johnboat, Raban faced such dangers as severe turbulence caused by the collision of a downstream current with an upstream wind; partially submerged jetties called wing dams that jut out from the banks to guide water into the main channel; waterlogged tree trunks barely floating just below the surface; huge boils, or domes of water, that swell up from the depths of the river; vicious whirlpools that form in eddies at bends in the river; and, of course, the wakes of monster towboats pushing acres of barges loaded with such cargoes as grain, iron ore, coal or gravel.

By comparison, a bicycle ride across the United States, seemed like a safe and simple undertaking.

As plans for our adventures progressed, we realized that our journeys would overlap for a time in the fall of 2009. What a bit of serendipity if we should meet!

We began to entertain the fanciful notion that, with the concurrence of the river and road gods, we might cross paths at St. Francisville in southeastern Louisiana.

St. Francisville, a jewel of a town in West Feliciana Parish, was the place where my fellow cyclists and I would cross the Mississippi River on our transcontinental journey along the southern tier of the United States. Neal, of course, would have to paddle past St. Francisville on his way to the Big Easy.

But our rendezvous on the river didn't take place at the time and place we had hoped for.

When my bicycling companions and I reached the Mississippi on Nov. 4, 2009, Neal was still further up the river in Mississippi doing video stories as an iReporter for CNN and for his blog, Flash River Safari.

We took a ferry across the Mississippi, a major milestone in our cross-country trek. I thought of Neal that day as we waited on the western bank for the ferry to take us across to St. Francisville.

The Mississippi, probably a mile wide at that point, is in the final stages of its 2,300-mile odyssey across the midsection of the United States. It has gathered water from 31 states and two Canadian provinces from the Rockies to the Appalachians, all funneling into feeder rivers along the way – the Wisconsin, the Illinois, the Missouri, the Ohio, the Arkansas and myriad others – and is rushing full bore to the sea.

For good reason, the Mississippi is called the Father of Waters.

After heavy rains upstream, the Mississippi was running high and fast that day, and two men in a canoe were riding the swift current downriver. Their craft seemed so frail on that mighty, mercurial river. I marveled at their skill and courage and was struck anew by the audacity of Neal's solo journey.

Although our rendezvous didn't occur when and where Neal and I had hoped for, when it did happen it was in a town very fitting for two people who have a deep association with and affection for the Mississippi: Hannibal, Mo., Mark Twain's boyhood home.

The graduation of a family friend from the University of Missouri at Columbia in May 2010 prompted a trip to Missouri. After the graduation, I drove to Hannibal.

Neal had been working on this book in Oxford, Miss., but he had decamped to Hannibal to tap the expertise of Cindy Lovell, executive director of the Mark Twain Boyhood Home & Museum.

"Dr. Moore, I presume," I said when I found Neal in the Java Jive coffee shop on Hannibal's Main Street. He had been hunched over his laptop working on his book amid the couches and easy chairs at the back of the shop.

Through Neal's good offices and Cindy's hospitality, I lodged in the Becky Thatcher Room at Cindy's rambling 1890s home filled with Twain memorabilia.

Cindy, a self-described "Twainiac" with encyclopedic knowledge of Twain and his times, has hung her favorite Twain quote above the door leading from the living room into the kitchen: "Let us endeavor so to live that when we come to die even the undertaker will be sorry."

During my brief visit to Hannibal, Neal and I walked along the waterfront as the rising Mississippi, swollen by seasonal flooding, crept up the brick-paved landing where steamboats once put in. We toured Twain's boyhood home and the nearby home of Tom Blankenship, son of the town drunk and an outcast from polite society who was the model for Huckleberry Finn.

We signed the whitewashed fence immortalized in *The Adventures of Tom Sawyer* and talked Twain with museum curator Henry Sweets.

We tramped through the cave where young Sam Clemens played and where Tom and Becky got lost.

That evening, we sat on Cindy's front porch swapping mostly true tales about our respective adventures, drank some robust but flat stout that I had schlepped in a growler from a brew pub in Columbia and watched as a large, well-fed raccoon repeatedly raided the bowls of food that Cindy had set out for the neighborhood cats.

When I was a boy, more than a century after Sam Clemens explored the woods and bluffs and caves about 90 miles upriver from my own hometown on the Mississippi, Tom and Huck were guiding spirits as I and my childhood friends pursued similar adventures in Alton.

In later life, I settled on a triumvirate of heroes, all Midwesterners: Mark Twain, Abe Lincoln and Harry Truman. But Twain was the one who has brought the most pleasure, inspired lame attempts at literary imitation and provided a fitting quote for many an occasion.

I affixed several of them, in fact, to pages in the blog that recorded my bicycle trip across America.

One of my favorites is from *The Innocents Abroad,* an account of Twain's travels in 1867 with other Americans through Europe and the Holy Land. It offers some sound reasons for venturing beyond the known and the comfortable:

"Travel is fatal to prejudice, bigotry, and narrow-mindedness, and many of our people need it sorely on these accounts. Broad, wholesome, charitable views of men and things cannot be acquired by vegetating in one little corner of the earth all one's lifetime."

So whether you do it by canoe or bicycle, RV or cruise liner, get out and move about the world. It's tonic for the soul.

—James R. Peipert, Fort Worth, 2012

EXPLANTORY

Each chapter is written as a singular story,
yet presented sequentially to tell the tale of the whole journey.
Corresponding passages by Mark Twain are inserted throughout
in appropriate transitions. These are indented and italicized.

Mississippi River

Areas, cities and towns featured in *Down the Mississippi*

LIGHTING OUT
FOR THE TERRITORY

ONE

A certain feeling of liberation…

THE TRIP FROM TAIPEI back to America was a sober awakening. I had planned and plotted for the previous six months, hitting the local gym and swimming lengths in the open sea, and yet I didn't feel ready. Taking myself out of my comfort zone – in this case *completely* out of my comfort zone – was a feeling my body wasn't accustomed to. I didn't listen to my body. Instead, I listened to my soul: to an insistent voice that started as a whisper and ended as a scream. There was no choice – I had to do it. I flew from Hong Kong up through China and

Russia and over the Bering Sea toward the North Pole. The impending adventure, I thought, would actually be a bit like going to the North Pole. I'd be transporting myself from a teeming Asian city, where the concept of "personal space" does not exist, to a place where, during much of the four months and 22 days that I would be on Mark Twain's river, I would not encounter a single living soul.

There's a certain feeling of liberation in stepping foot for the first time into one of the world's great cities. I've traveled to New York, to Cairo, to Cape Town, to the jungles of Southeast Asia. You spin the globe and put your best foot forward, often with little to no money in your pockets. You're forced to meet the locals, take a job, get into the rhythm of the city and figure out how its characters operate. Every town has a heartbeat, an ebb and flow. The best approach is to take up residence in the city center, to watch the cycle of the workday, to meet the street characters, the club regulars, the fellow travelers in the hotel that caters to the itinerant Bohemians. There's always an iconic eatery or historic coffee shop where old-timers swap stories, where the wise old men of the city come to drink tea and smoke hookah pipes and tell you about better days, about how the town operated in past times, about who its bosses were then. In every city there are children on the street, the future reflected in their faces. You lounge around in the great cafes of the world, with or without a cup or glass in your hand, and take it all in. And if you're lucky, a lady of the night might come along and sing you a song, and maybe not charge too much for the tune.

When I find a well-drawn character in fiction or biography I generally take a warm personal interest in him, for the reason that I have known him before – met him on the river.

—*Life on the Mississippi,* 1883, Chapter 18

It was during one of these soul-searching sojourns on the other side of the globe – during a time when the pundits, bankers and politicians were sounding alarm and headlines predicted economic collapse – when the epiphany occurred.

It was at first light, a predawn morning in Cape Town, when I realized I could do it. I could return to my home country, launch a canoe at the source of the Mississippi River, paddle it downstream, and find firsthand the stories that would tell the true tale. The Mississippi is not just any river. It's one of the world's greatest and most majestic thoroughfares, a storied road through the heart of America.

I would be nowhere near the Sahara, or Old Delhi, or Pamplona. Yet I knew that this river, Twain's river, would take me on the greatest adventure of my life. I would replicate my previous journeys in a single setting, on the river whose name I learned to spell in sing-song fashion as a child, but whose waters I had yet to explore. I pulled out a map and found that 10 states and hundreds of towns lie along its serpentine course to the Gulf of Mexico. I knew that each town would have its own rhyme and reason, its own personality, its singular past, present and future. Each river stop would present its share of bubbas and gossips, singers and artisans, scorekeepers and politicians, all sharing that human desire to flourish, rooted in the need to survive. I wanted to hear their versions of events, witness their responses and decipher their hopes. If I could listen carefully, edit sparingly, and speak softly, I just might put a human face on this growing economic calamity. I would ask them to tell their own stories.

If you wish to lower yourself in a person's favor, one good way is to tell his story over again, the way you heard it.

—*Mark Twain's Notebook,* 1898

This great river slices the nation from north to south and separates its east and west. It is the lifeblood of America and it pulsates with her hopes and dreams. But folks who live along the Mississippi know the despair that the river can bring. Hundred-year floods have inundated their land twice in the span of a decade. Her characters have performed in classic American tragedies, black comedies and the occasional Broadway musical. If ever an avenue was worth exploring in search of un-whitewashed testimony on the soul of America, the Mississippi River is more than worthy as a candidate. Those who dwell along her banks possess the pluck and fortitude of our forefathers, akin to a brash pride. If any Americans could give a true account of their nation's situation, it would be those along the Mississippi, whose grit and tenacity is the stuff of lore.

> *The man they called Ed said the muddy Mississippi water was wholesomer to drink than the clear water of the Ohio; he said if you let a pint of this yaller Mississippi water settle, you would have about a half to three-quarters of an inch of mud in the bottom, according to the stage of the river, and then it warn't no better than Ohio water - what you wanted to do was to keep it stirred up - and when the river was low, keep mud on hand to put in and thicken the water up the way it ought to be.*

> *The Child of Calamity said that was so; he said there was nutritiousness in the mud, and a man that drunk Mississippi water could grow corn in his stomach if he wanted to. He says:*

> *"You look at the graveyards; that tells the tale. Trees won't grow worth shucks in a Cincinnati graveyard, but in a Sent Louis graveyard they grow upwards of eight hundred foot high. It's all on account of the water the people drunk before they laid up. A Cincinnati corpse don't richen a soil any."*

—*Life on the Mississippi,* 1883, Chapter 3

As a traveler you spend a lot of time with fellow expatriates, often in exotic locales, imagining the perfect trip, one on which you "put yourself out there," pushing your body and mind to their limits. But putting myself "out there" was a new concept in my life that, in the end,

31

had to come from within. To put myself purposefully in a situation where there would be no promises – no certainty of survival, no assurance of shelter, no one to prop me up save for myself drove home the knowledge that my trust would be placed in a river, a river with which I would have to become intimate in order to succeed.

Canoeing the Mississippi makes me think of the old cliché: There's a fine line between genius and insanity. Some folks would tip their hats to you, seeing the journey as a reflection of the American spirit. Others would berate you as a vagabond. And still others would flat out tell you that you were going to die.

In the end, you have to listen to your own voice – will yourself to make it, to survive the hard times and to see yourself through. From the beginning, I saw myself as a traveling Candide, as a Huckleberry Finn of sorts – in the sense that I had no cares, no set itinerary, no place that I had to get myself to. The search for those "positive American stories" was the only order of the day. I wanted to viscerally touch America by traveling down her central corridor. I would document the lives I encountered all the way down. When asked how I planned to handle the dangers of this not-too-gentle river, my response to friends and myself was simple: put myself on the river and, come what may – hell or high water, peril or paradise – I'd have no choice but to confront it and experience it all. And if

I were lucky, I'd live to tell the tale. Laden with the latest technology – cameras, laptop and MiFi wireless wizardry – I would report for CNN as a "citizen journalist" along the way, shooting and writing and uploading stories when and where I could, and, in the best of times, from my own canoe.

Courage is resistance to fear, mastery of fear – not absence of fear.

—*Pudd'nhead Wilson's Calendar,* 1894

At long last, the day and hour of my planned launch arrived, and there I was, on the shores of Lake Itasca in Minnesota's Wild North. I had pictured my departure, my great getaway into nature, as a rather momentous event. But it turned out not to be exactly so. The launch bordered on the comical because I had to shoot the video introducing my expedition all by myself, and, as things turned out, that sorry episode made me look like a bumbling fool. My niece, who is a soil scientist in the general area, and her son, my great-nephew, had dropped me off, taken my picture and shaken hands. Then they were off.

I had wanted to be on my own to shoot the video because I was nervous about the whole enterprise at this point and full of nervous energy. I had selected a portion of Lake Itasca that I thought was picturesque enough, yet not so busy as the official launching wharf.

I was happy with my choice – that is, until a member

of the local forestry service showed up with an ear-splitting, hand-held sand-sweeping machine, followed by an abundance of young families who had come up from Minneapolis-St. Paul to lie on the sand and splash around in the lake. Having set up the shot for my opening monologue, I had no choice but to stand amid the families' chatter to deliver my salutational speech of conquest – of course before I had conquered anything. I hit "record" on my laptop's iSight, stole an awkward glance at the forestry personnel now congregated at my side, glanced again at the moms and kids just in front of me, stepped in front of my canoe, cleared my throat and intoned in my best TV voice:

> Hi, my name is Neal Moore, and I'm an international citizen journalist for CNN. I'm going to be launching from here at Lake Itasca, Minnesota, for the journey of a lifetime. The game plan: to canoe the entire length of the Mississippi River from here at the headwaters all the way down to New Orleans, Louisiana, stopping off to find and highlight positive American stories meets planned community projects in association with the Creative Visions Foundation. The destination: Middle America – the very heart and soul of America, at her finest.

The speech was pretty straightforward and should have taken two or three takes for a wrap, but with this ready-made audience, combined with my own reluctance to actually get into the canoe, it took between 20 and 30. That turned out to be OK, however, because, after my 15th take, the people all around simply ignored me, shaking their heads in frustration, dismissing me as the nut that I obviously was.

With video clip complete, I attempted to pack up the canoe with all of my gear – an equally daunting prospect considering I clearly had far too much gear to fit comfortably into my 16-foot canoe. A young man named Bjorn and his girlfriend introduced themselves and wished me luck. They had overheard the monologue – several times, as they pointed out – and were keen to follow my trip online and to meet up in person if possible when I got to Minneapolis. We shook hands and exchanged contact information and then I went back to packing the canoe. Configuring the bags in different ways I was able to at long last to make it all fit, with barely room for myself. This was the moment when I put on my French Foreign Legion hat, grabbed my vintage 1960s Old Town paddle, and climbed in – taking care not to tip the boat. The gentle lapping of the lake's small waves was keeping the canoe against the shore, so I brought the paddle down to push off. A lady with a camera came over to snap a picture. I smiled and paddled and then I was free, out in the lake with the headwaters in sight directly ahead.

It's hard to explain in words what I felt, out on my own in the center of the lake. The moment when I placed the canoe into the water, with all of my worldly possessions, hopped in, and began to paddle out to the center of Lake Itasca was the moment everything changed. At once, all of the stress washed off me, all of my apprehension about surviving with nature, all of my pre-conceived notions that I might not make it. I smiled a great smile – a smile that I had not smiled ever in my life. It wasn't a smile of achievement or of love or of triumph; it was a smile of self-confidence, of making it past a personal trial and beating it. At the moment when the stress left me, I knew that I not only *could* make it, but *would,* make it – that I would indeed make it all the way down to New Orleans. I think in retrospect it was a smile of complete freedom.

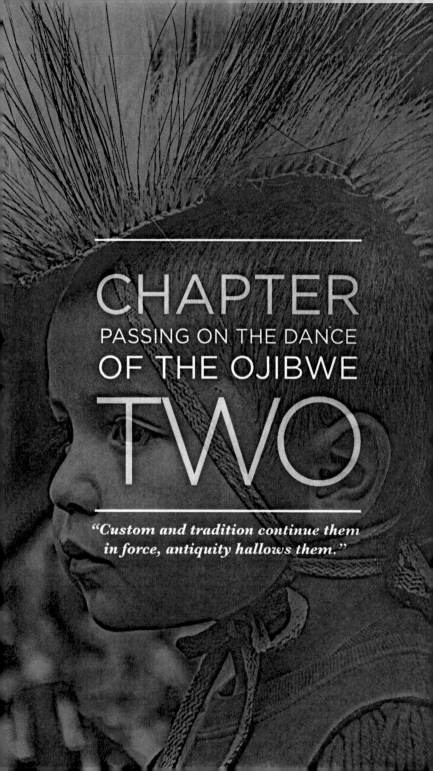

CHAPTER
PASSING ON THE DANCE
OF THE OJIBWE
TWO

"Custom and tradition continue them in force, antiquity hallows them."

“THE HEADWATERS” IS A GROUP of rocks
designated as "the source" of the Mississippi River –
strung out across the place where the water flows out
of Lake Itasca to form the river, really just a stream at that
point. It's a spot for tourists to gather and take pictures.
As I paddled my canoe up to the headwaters, where I would
have to portage my canoe and gear, a family of tourists
came along and asked what I was up to and if they could
help. I told them that I was "doing the river" and that if
they wanted to help, they certainly could. Still smiling,

I grabbed one bag and they grabbed the rest. The sun was at full height, lording itself high above this first day of pure bliss, the sort of day when you want to get outside to see some sights and take it all in. I was heaving the oversized, blue river bag when I turned around and, to my amazement, saw that the father was portaging the canoe. A portage of gear and canoe that would have taken several trips turned out to take only one. As the canoe was set gently into the fledgling river, a brisk walk down a dirt path, I got in, turned and snapped a picture of the group. Just downstream from the headwaters I came upon a family of ducks, a flare of bright blue gracing the mother's wing as her troop of ducklings followed dutifully behind.

The sun was now baking hot and I pulled under the second footbridge I came to for a little respite from the sun. I tied up underneath, on the left bank, and broke out my laptop computer to edit the video of the launch and to try to upload it. As I was busy fiddling with my electronic gear, a platoon of boys in swimming trunks came marching through, so busy splashing along the stream that they didn't notice me. The river is very narrow here and it struck me as odd that they had missed me. About an hour later, when I had edited my opening monologue and found that I didn't have a wireless signal strong enough to upload video from this location, the boys came back, this time looking directly at me. There's something magical about youth in connection with this river, about the sprightliness of the boys, away from their parents and all adults in the middle of summer, free from academic responsibility. I would later see fishermen of all ages along the river and knew that their presence was a compliment to the river herself. Those who were lucky enough to grow up along the Mississippi's banks would fish her as children, through their teenage years, into adulthood, and later to the cusp of their mortality. These boys, who would have been local, must have been a couple years into double digits. They stopped their horseplay long enough to nod toward me and ask if I was a photographer. With a big Nikon camera slung around my neck, I nodded yes, and they were gone. The scene embarrassed me because I realized that I shouldn't have had the camera and computer gadgetry out like that – that it was an affront to the nature sparkling so brightly all around me, that it would detract from a scene of immense beauty rather than underscore and highlight it. That, in fact, some things don't need to be highlighted; that they're just fine and wondrous all on their own.

Nine days of intense paddling downriver from Lake Itasca brought me to the Leech Lake Band of the Ojibwe, the indigenous American people who gave the Mississippi its name. Linguists and historians tell us that *Mississippi* is derived from the Ojibwe word *misi-ziibi,* or "great river."

All this part of the river is rich in Indian history and traditions. Black Hawk's was once a puissant name hereabouts; as was Keokuk's, further down. A few miles below Dubuque is the Tete de Mort Death's-head rock, or bluff – to the top of which the French drove a band of Indians, in early times, and cooped them up there, with death for a certainty, and only the manner of it matter of choice – to starve, or jump off and kill themselves.

—*Life on the Mississippi*, 1883, Chapter 58

At this stage of the journey, I was looking for basic themes for my stories, not yet fully understanding that sentiment in nearly every town would swirl around a common cause. If I could discern the core themes of these towns and the players who generate them, I could find the stories and their tellers and be in a position to share them.

The night before an Ojibwe powwow I was taken to meet the elder responsible for the event, an 87-year-old gentleman named John Mitchell. The tribal elder was sitting by an outdoor fire on the reservation where the powwow was to take place. He stepped away from his chair to smile and to shake my hand. Fresh wood was piled on the fire and the smoke was simultaneously intoxicating and mystifying. I was honored and delighted to be there. It was a strange feeling, one I would describe as reverence. Surprisingly, I didn't feel like the outsider that I obviously was. I felt accepted, and there was a warmth to the whole scene that had nothing to do with the fire, although on that unseasonably brisk evening it must have been a contributing factor. I'm not exactly a spiritual person, so it's odd that I would describe it in this way, but the happiness seemed to be coming from within, not only from within myself but from those all around – as if anticipation of the event that was about to take place was contagious. Vintage campers and pickup trucks with reservation plates were parked in the surrounding woods. Families who had traveled from near and far were circling their own family campfires, gossiping, laughing, smoking, drumming and singing. It was already late and I felt guilty to be taking the elder's time at such an hour, but he seemed keen to share a word. I plunged in with my scripted questions:

"Can you tell me how the art of the Ojibwe dance is passed down from generation to generation?" I asked.

"No," responded Mitchell, leaning forward, taking his time before continuing. "You have to come here tomorrow and watch and listen and *feel* – and then you will know for yourself how the dance is passed on. This is how it is for all. It is not a thing that can be taught – it doesn't work that way." I understood what the elder meant and I felt like an idiot. The dance and culture were more than things that could be taught; they had to be absorbed. This was sacred.

Custom and tradition continue them in force, antiquity hallows them.

—*Following the Equator*, 1897, Chapter 40

I asked Mitchell if I could interview him the next day. He just laughed and said that he would have nothing important to say. "You don't want to interview me. You want to interview Bob Gotchie here. This is a man with answers. This is the man that is really running the show."

Bob Gotchie is a council member who had been assigned to be my guide by council chairman, Milt Gotchie. The two Gotchies were related, as was Mitchell. Bob was the youngest of the trio, a hardened fellow who had seen and lived much but had now mellowed and was all about the tribe – and the powwow. He was quick to smile and to shake my hand, and by the way he brushed off Mitchell's compliment, I could tell that he was a man of humility – a man who had nothing to prove.

I thanked Mitchell for his time and Bob Gotchie walked me over toward a rambling community building of sorts, just to the side of the powwow ring.

"John just won the National Elder Teacher of the Year Award, an award voted on by 500 tribes across the country," explained Bob, which of course made perfect sense. John Mitchell was kind in his method of instruction.

"You're going to see a lot of people using tobacco here," Bob said as we walked past several young girls laughing, giggling and holding hands while indulging in the art of the smoke. "It's part of our tradition – a part of our culture."

"Here, you can come in and we can talk," Bob said as we

got to the building. The back door was locked so we went to the side door, walking up a long, wooden ramp. The first thing that caught my eye inside was a bright green painting of the powwow ring with dancers in full dance regalia. The setting of the painting seemed timeless. It depicted a scene that could have played out 200 years ago, but the painting looked new. Bob told me that the painting was new but that it represented a tradition going back generations, centuries. I looked out the window next to the painting and saw the same scene – the sacred powwow ring.

A youngster came up the steps from downstairs and greeted Bob with a reverence that reinforced my feeling that he was someone of importance who has earned respect. We walked down the steps and found a couple of couches in a far corner. We sat across from each other, and as Bob began to talk, I took out my notebook and began to scrawl notes.

One thing that struck me immediately was a sense of humility in the characters of John Mitchell and both of the Gotchies. It wasn't something put on for a visitor; it was the genuine article, something that I admired and wished that I had myself. When Bob launched into his story I knew that we would be here for some time. He told me about his youth and how he had become a hardened young man – "like many young men here on the reservation" – and how he had spent time in jail. I didn't ask about his crime. Whatever it was, it didn't seem to define the man before me. He said that he had paid his debt to society and moved on. Then he laughed, shook his head and began to cry. We were well into our conversation when it happened. I was taken aback. I would have sworn that a man like Bob Gotchie would never cry, although this would be a sign of reverence and humility that I would encounter again with the Ojibwe. That brief interruption in Bob's narrative came when he was telling me about one of his early influences, about an aunt whom he described as "a real hard case."

"We'd be running wild," recalled Bob, "running wild as boys will do and she'd come and she'd get us all riled up and excited about the powwow." Bob told the story as if his aunt were right there in front of him again. He was looking forward, straight through me, and I could tell that he was peering into a different time. "'You know the powwow is coming,' and we'd say, 'Yeah, we know.' She'd be yelling and cussing and telling us we had to sort ourselves out and get ourselves in line." Bob broke down during the story. When he had the power to speak again he told me that it was for her he would dance. That it was the same today as it was when he was a boy. "You know, it's funny – I'm going to all this work year in and year out just to make her proud. Even though she's been gone for several years now, I can still hear her sing."

After breakfast his aunt took him aside, and Tom almost brightened in the hope that he was going to be flogged; but it was not so. His aunt wept over him and asked him how he could go and break her old heart so; and finally told him to go on, and ruin himself and bring her gray hairs with sorrow to the grave, for it was no use for her to try anymore. This was worse than a thousand whippings, and Tom's heart was sorer now than his body. He cried, he pleaded for forgiveness, promised to reform over and over again, and then received his dismissal, feeling that he had won but an imperfect forgiveness and established but a feeble confidence.

—*The Adventures of Tom Sawyer*, 1876, Chapter 10

"You're going to see a number of things tomorrow you've never seen before. So I'm going to tell you about it so you'll know what you're witnessing," Bob said.

I nodded my head and continued to scribble.

"Children will come and throw money at the feet of the dancers while they are dancing. This is to show respect for the dance and for the dancers, as well as to show people their favorites. The money is then collected and brought to the elders' booth – as a sign of respect to our elders. This is what the whole powwow is really about. It is here that we honor our veterans, that we honor our elders, that we honor our women, that we honor our youth."

They honor everybody, I thought. What a great idea – to highlight the positive in everybody.

"At 1 p.m. you're going to see the grand entry," Bob continued. "The elders are going to come first and they are going to carry the eagle staff. They are going to honor the vets of all the wars. We then honor the royalties, both local and visiting, and then we go into the dances. Out of all of the boys we will choose a new brave and out of all the girls, a new princess."

I had read that the powwow of the Leech Lake Band of Ojibwe stood out because it featured 300 dancers, all in full regalia, and that it included the old and the young.

"How many dancers do you expect? Could it be more than 300?" I asked.

Bob was an optimist. He smiled and said, "Who knows – that's the beauty. It could be 300 dancers out there tomorrow or it could be a thousand. One thing for sure, the powwow is growing every year." I looked out the window from where we sat and I could feel it, too. There was the powwow ring with the fire and the smoke, and the people walking in groups, everybody smiling. Absolutely anything was possible. It was a great feeling.

"There are songs that are sacred that cannot be recorded by camera or sound," Bob said. "For example, each traditional drum has within it a song that only that drum can play, that belongs to that particular drum. You will hear four opening songs once the dancers have danced their opening dance. There are also sacred dances, but we'll get to that at a later time. When these songs are played, and when the sacred dances are danced, you need to turn off your camera."

I nodded in wonder and amazement. This was a ritual that I had never heard of, but it has been practiced as far back as the Ojibwe can remember. I said out loud so that Bob would know that I understood: "Before I shoot a song or record a dance, I'll get the green light first."

"There will be somebody with you."

I asked if the Ojibwe people were able to get by financially. He said that it was a tough go, that he could make more money off the reservation than on it, but that he belonged here and that this was part of what the powwow is about. It was about a reason for his people to come together; it was a time of celebration. I looked at my watch and saw that it was midnight. I was humbled that this man had spent so much time with me. Bob wanted me to understand the powwow and he wanted me to get it right. He didn't have to take the time that he did, but he had, and he had done it out of love. His description of the powwow and what I was to experience the next day was not so much a briefing for a visiting journalist, but the sharing of a sacred story between friends. We had been talking for several hours.

The following afternoon I met Milt Gotchie at his office beside the powwow ring. He was being pulled in all directions, so he pointed across the bleachers to where Bob was supervising some electrical work. I smiled and waved a thank-you. As I walked toward Bob, I took in the many kiosks encircling the bleachers of the powwow ring. Families would be selling kettle corn and Indian fry bread while others would display tanned animal hides and feathers. One woman at a T-shirt kiosk scrutinized a $20 bill for signs that it was counterfeit. The 21st-century economy was nothing new to these people.

Bob was holding some wires along with another man in the Wild Rice Soup kiosk and he called out a greeting when he saw me. He patted me on the back with his free hand and asked if I'd ever tried "real Ojibwe wild rice soup." When I shook my head no, the woman behind the counter began to work her magic.

Just steps away dancers of all ages began to line up to get credentials for the powwow, the numbers that would identify them as official "competition" dancers for various events. As the woman handed me a steaming bowl of soup, Bob explained the order of the dances for the afternoon.

"Following the grand entry and the royalties will come the men's traditional dancers, the men's non-bustle, men's grass dancers, ladies' traditional dancers, ladies' jingle dress (healing dress), ladies' fancy shells, followed in turn by the boys and then girls."

As the bleachers began to fill, there was more activity outside the ring than within. Most of the men around the fires sported tattoos and bandanas, and some had feathers sprouting from their hair and bandanas. As I looked closer,

I noticed one man with the real head of a black bear perched atop his own head. Many of the women held eagles' wings to their chests and boys clutched staffs with sharp eagle talons at the ends. I was thinking that the creatures of the wild represented in these totems were the "power animals" of the people who wore them, spirits to empower them or to protect them from harm. I suddenly recognized what a daunting prospect it would be to correctly chronicle this powwow.

I asked if it would be appropriate to interview the various groups of people on the sidelines and Bob replied, "Oh sure. People are going to poke fun at you. Oh, are they going to poke fun at you! But just roll with it and laugh along with them. They will like you and they will mean you no harm. Go right ahead. I'll catch up to you later."

The nervous, dapper, "peart" young man took the chair I offered him, and said he was connected with the Daily Thunderstorm, *and added, –*

"Hoping it's no harm, I've come to interview you."

"Come to what?"

"Interview you."

—*Encounter with an interviewer,* 1874

As I walked forward, I passed several groups of Ojibwe before gathering the courage to approach one. I challenged myself to speak to the toughest-looking of the lot. A mustache accentuated his broken nose, and sunglasses concealed his eyes. The bandana tied around his head held several feathers, with a multicolored stick running through the headgear like an arrow. Tattoos rounded out the look. I approached and asked if I could ask some questions. He gave his assent.

"What is special about this powwow?"

"This is Mii-Gwitch Mahnomen Days," replied the broken- nosed dancer, referring to the annual July festival whose name translates roughly as "Thank you, wild rice." Speaking from the heart, speaking with surprising conviction, he said, "We are thankful for the wild rice that we harvest every year. We start next month. This is a blessing for the bounty we're going to be getting in. We've been doing this for ... centuries, as far as I know. We also thank the Great Spirits for all the things they have given us in our life. Our ancestors have done it, we've done it, and we're doing it now today."

With one interview completed, I thanked him and walked away with newfound confidence, eager to gather more stories. As I walked along the outer ring, a solitary man caught my eye. He was leaning on the boundary bars, looking in toward the ring. A folded American flag was tucked under one arm, and he was decked out in a combination of military fatigues and traditional Ojibwe dance regalia.

"Can I ask you a few questions?" I said.

"Sure," he said. But when I reached into my shoulder bag to take out my video camera, the man blocked it with his fist and said, "I said you could ask questions, but not with a camera." A hearty laugh told me that he wasn't upset. It also told me that what he had to say would be important.

"Sorry about that. We can do it that way, too," I replied, taking out my notebook and pen.

"These poles that line the powwow ring are power rings," the man explained. "Families bring a flag to honor all the veterans. It takes a veteran to raise a flag."

His name was Don Schaaf, and he had seen combat as a Marine in Beirut.

"This local Ball Club day is a healing day," he said, referring to the Ojibwe town called Ball Club, named for a kind of wooden war club with a ball at the end. "It is a day to socialize – to come together. All the families in this community come together. I am here to raise a flag for my father. His name was Al Schaaf, and he fell as a paratrooper in Korea."

I told Schaaf that I was sorry for his father. He continued to look out onto the ring, as if he had been anticipating this moment all year, as if he were communicating with his father. But then, speaking for the tribe as a whole, he said, "We've lost young and old. It's basically how we grieve and how we deal."

I walked along and had begun to film a trio of female

elders when one put her hand up and stopped me again.

"No, not on the camera. I am sorry," the woman said.

I had asked permission before starting to film, but she hadn't understood my intention. I would later learn that it was important to obtain clear permission before filming anyone here at Ball Club, as some believe that capturing their image with a camera is, in fact, stealing their power.

At the other extreme, several children who had seen my camera took me by the hand and brought me over to their family campfire, where they demanded to be interviewed. I asked an older woman sitting beside the fire if she was related to the children and if it was OK to talk to them.

"Yes, I am the grandmother," she said.

The kids were gregarious and boastful, and they explained to me, amid puffs of cigarette smoke, that they had all traveled from Duluth, on the western end of Lake Superior. When I would ask one kid a question, the older sister, age 13, would answer for everybody. She would expect me to swing the camera her way whenever she would answer for her younger siblings. If I didn't, she would simply whisper into the ear of the sibling being interviewed just loud enough to be heard. The children would squeal with delight at the attention and at their answers. What I learned from these kids is that various bands of Ojibwe travel to powwows throughout the summer, transporting themselves all over this part of the United States and even up into Canada, to all the places where Ojibwe can be found.

I positioned myself under the announcer's box, just inside the perimeter of the powwow ring. Electricity was in the air as the lead dancers came into the ring, stomping to the beat of the drum. This was the grand entry, and the most senior veteran, out front and center, turned out to be another Gotchie, whose first name was Sandy. He sported a cap that said "WWII VETERAN" and he carried a large staff in one hand and a set of feathered hoops in the other. Other than the hat, he wore traditional Ojibwe garb complete with a vest adorned with depictions of bear paws. On one hand he wore a brown leather glove, and I wondered if it covered a war deformity. He was surrounded by warriors, military men whose service extended back through several wars. Some faces were painted blue and black. Feathers were everywhere – atop the warriors' heads, springing from their backs, decorating their staffs and along the side of a bright-red banner that read: "LEECH LAKE NATION."

The warriors danced forward and American flags were raised. The flag-raising was followed by a series of drum sessions, two of which I was able to chronicle. Different clans of the Ojibwe people set up within the powwow ring. The drummers were all male, of all ages. A toddler, sitting on the lap of his uncle, peered intently at the gargantuan drum as his family yelled and beat and sang.

"It's important to us as a people," explained a young

father who had brought his wife and baby girl. "When you hear that drumbeat, it always brings us back to being in the womb of our mother. My daughter here is brand-new and she really enjoys being here. It's a calming feeling for her; it's a positive experience." The baby girl, clutching the beaded necklace of her mother, looked about in wonder.

I asked one woman the size of her family.

"Twelve girls and four boys," the woman answered, her head held high. "Sixty some grandkids and 38 great-grandkids."

One of the grandchildren, Andrew Wakonabo, had earned the title of Brave of the Year of the Leech Lake Band of Ojibwe for 2008.

When the boy danced, he stood out from the pack, not because he wore a ribbon over his shoulder that proclaimed his title within the tribe. There was a natural dignity to his movements as his head bobbed in time to the chants, his arms floating out effortlessly in either direction. The dance was all his own.

I was granted an interview after the boy's final dance, his family encouraging him with smiles of honor and respect. His mother had taken off his multicolored feathered headdress, but he still wore the rest of his Ojibwe garb, including the ribbon.

"Can you tell us, when you become a brave – what happens?" I asked.

Andrew smiled before answering. "You have to go to every

powwow, pretty much, and represent the town that you won brave in."

Bob Gotchie had explained the previous night that to win the title of brave or princess is a great honor, something to aspire to, much more than just the judging of the dance.

"The youngsters have to meet a certain standard in their personal lives and they have to uphold that standard for the entire year," he had said. "They must demonstrate responsibilities so that other youth look up to them. They directly represent the nation."

Andrew Wakonabo was different from the other young people I had talked to earlier that day. He answered my questions with thought and dignity, and although his whole family was right there, he answered the questions by himself.

"I pretty much learned myself – watching other people dance," he explained. "I feel good when I dance."

There is a bond between the old and the young in the Native-American community that other cultures can learn from. The Ojibwe historically used intricate pictures on birch bark scrolls to transmit knowledge. This day, I learned that for the Ojibwe, dance communicates love – love of family, love of culture and a love of tradition. The value of the dance, explained an older member of the Leech Lake Band of Ojibwe, "is impossible to put into words."

CHAPTER

CARPE
DIEM
THREE

Independent Age newspaper display in Aitkin, Minn.

I T WAS ABOUT 4:30 p.m. on Tuesday, July 14, when the town siren went off in Blackduck, Minn. Everyone is familiar with the siren here because the town tests it every day at noon. But in late afternoon, the siren was unexpected. It sounded for a long time, its insistent wail competing with the rain and wind outside the house where I was staying. I felt a tinge of apprehension. I imagined a fire in the small business district or, maybe, just a cat stuck up in a tree. Thinking I might witness a rescue of some kind, I grabbed my cameras and hurried for my niece's car.

The Mississippi embarks on a circuitous northeasterly course when it trickles out of Lake Itasca and begins its 2,300-mile journey to the Gulf of Mexico. I had been off the river for a day, holed up in my niece's house in Blackduck, about 25 miles northeast of Bemidji, the first town of any size along the Mississippi. I had been drying out my clothes and gear and preparing for a rare treat – a home stay with extended family, just off the river.

A fire engine and police cars rushed through town as curious residents watched from the sidewalks. As I approached a stop sign before turning onto a westbound road, I saw three or four other cars and trucks following the emergency vehicles. We were all headed in the same direction. What I didn't know at the time was that the town siren hadn't sounded for an emergency for some time and that these local people weren't following the emergency vehicles to gawk or to take pictures. They were going to help.

Soon I saw in the rearview mirror a four-wheel-drive vehicle from the sheriff's department racing up behind me. I pulled to the side and saw that the vehicle was towing a speedboat. Then I knew. The emergency was on Blackduck Lake, due west of the town, about a mile off the highway.

I found a dirt road away from the other vehicles and I got out of the car to take a look. The area between the lake and where I had parked was all reeds and muck. But it was the closest to the lake that I could get without being in the way. I asked a fireman who approached on foot what had happened and if I could help.

"Boating accident – two bodies in the water," he said. "I'm going to search the shore here in the reeds. They could have tried to swim."

We tried to wade out into the reeds but the muck was thick. Then I looked to the top of my niece's car and saw my canoe. Inside were my paddles, which I had left in the car the night before after my niece had brought me to her house from the river.

A local resident came along and helped me launch the canoe from a private dock. Lots of bigger boats were out on the water, but I saw no other canoes that could penetrate the reeds and cattails. I then was told that the owner of the house whose dock I had used had launched her kayak. I followed her onto the lake.

The water was choppy, but amid the cattails I could keep my course, grabbing onto them when necessary to balance the canoe. I had searched along the shore for about two hours when the wind picked up and the waves became dangerously choppy. I was headed back to the dock when I saw a blue boat almost completely submerged, surrounded by rescue craft from the Beltrami County sheriff's department. The feeling of foreboding that haunted the day gave way to sickening resignation, acceptance of reality.

The two people lost on the lake were not going to be

rescued. The sheriff's deputies around the capsized pleasure craft set out orange buoys so divers would know where to start their search. The search was called off for the night shortly thereafter as the weather again took a turn for the worse. The wind picked up and showed no signs of relenting.

I didn't report on this story and I didn't take pictures. I only recounted what I experienced a couple of days later because I was impressed by how the people of Blackduck banded together. This is what people do. Without thinking, without planning, operating on instinct. This could be Anytown, U.S.A., and the reaction to an emergency would be much the same. The other, more personal, reason for not reporting on the lake accident at the time was the melancholy and reflection that it prompted. Small craft and bad weather make for a dangerous combination. That might be me the rescue boats are looking for one day. I couldn't sleep for at least two nights.

That afternoon in Blackduck, I was in the right place at the right time, or the wrong place at the wrong time. Launching my canoe on the lake was no more heroic than stopping at a red light. I couldn't count the boats out there – all sizes, all searching, all trying to help. I had joined a community that was coming together, clinging to the hope that we may yet flourish through adversity. We may find a lost child, put out a fire, build a new school, save the day. People everywhere do it everyday. Even though we don't win them all, we don't stop trying.

The searchers' faces told all. We would simply look at each other and nod. Others without boats were in the reeds in their wetsuits. I read in the paper a couple days later that other locals had prepared food and coffee for the searchers. Still others came to comfort the mother of one of the missing young men. She had come to the lake, shouting his name late into the night.

The water has lured countless numbers to their deaths, whether on Blackduck Lake or the Mississippi River. The fragility of life and the broken hearts of the grieving are as timeless as the sunrise. In 1858, the Memphis *Eagle and Enquirer* reported on a young man who arrived at a makeshift hospital to find his younger brother fast approaching death from a boiler explosion on a steamboat, an accident all too common in those times: "He hurried to the Exchange to see his brother, and on approaching the bedside of the wounded man, his feelings so much overcame him, at the scalded and emaciated form before him, that he sunk to the floor overpowered. There was scarcely a dry eye in the house; the poor sufferers shed tears at the sight." That big brother was Samuel Clemens, the cub pilot who would later become Mark Twain. Death is indiscriminate. All are touched; none are spared.

I found Henry stretched upon a mattress on the floor of a great building, along with thirty or forty other scalded and wounded persons, and was promptly informed, by some indiscreet person, that he had inhaled steam, that his body was badly scalded, and that he would live but a little while; also, I was told that the physicians and nurses were giving their whole attention to persons who had a chance of being saved. They were short-handed in the matter of physicians and nurses, and Henry and such others as were considered to be fatally hurt were receiving only such attention as could be spared, from time to time, from the more urgent cases.

—*The Autobiography of Mark Twain,* (13th edition, edited by Charles Neider), 1977, Chapter 20

Two young men, Justin Daryl Anderson and Cody James Krueger, both 21, *had* been rescued by locals shortly after the accident on Blackduck Lake, caused by a freak, five-foot wave. The bodies of Adam Joseph Bobick, 26, and Shawn Allen Ramsdell, 33, both of Little Falls, Minn., were recovered the next day.

Although this wasn't the sort of "positive American story" I hoped to find when I set out on my feel-good safari, I was reminded again, unnecessarily, that each of us is one heartbeat away from this sort of story. It is our action – or inaction – that make the tale worth sharing.

A couple of nights later, I sat on a porch swing with my niece, drinking beer, while my 12-year-old great-nephew ran from sprinkler to sprinkler on a lawn that stretched into the wilderness. We talked that night about life and death, about the fact that I had been an absentee uncle, always on the periphery, out there somewhere in the big wide world. I didn't want to say goodbye, and it was a tough ride back to the river when the time came, racing down a dirt road, trying to reach the Mississippi before sunset. I took my time unloading the station wagon as young Forest collected frogs along the shore. We had become closer during this visit than during any other. A big part of it, I think, was the setting – the outdoors. Or it could have been the accident on the lake and the reminders to cherish what matters. And then I was off, paddling downstream in search of Gambler's Point, a canoe-only campsite just around the bend.

> *[A] family brought love, and distributed it among many objects, and intensified it, and this engendered wearing cares and anxieties, and when the objects suffered or died the miseries and anxieties multiplied and broke the heart and shortened life...*

—*The Mysterious Stranger*, 1916

By the time I pulled into the town of Aitkin, I had grown a beard. At least it was the longest beard I'd ever taken time to cultivate. It had been about a week since my niece had brought me back to the Mississippi. But by this time I was only vaguely aware of how many days I'd been on the river, and I was no longer certain what day of the week it was. It wasn't that keeping track of the days of the week had lost importance. It was that the days had taken on a different sort of significance. I was really living, and everything felt more important than ever before.

I sensed a nervous excitement rumbling inside me as I neared civilization, as I came within striking distance of a town. My progress at this stage of the journey was about 10 miles for every three hours of paddling. So my approach to a town and perhaps a greasy-spoon café was cause for celebration. Some landmarks along the river match up with the map – a nearby highway, a bridge, a sharp turn in the river. You take courage with such a sight, affirmation that you're about where you expect to be. You quicken the pace of your paddling, unconsciously whistling, befriending the wildlife all around. The rule is that by paddling you earn these river towns and that, as a journalist, you earn their stories – story ideas that rattle around in your head for days before you actually arrive. Then again, there are the places you stumble upon, the unanticipated stories that present themselves, begging to be told.

My article was about the burning of the clipper-ship 'Hornet' on the line, May 3, 1866. There were thirty-one men on board at the time, and I was in Honolulu when the fifteen lean and ghostly survivors arrived there after a voyage of forty-three days in an open boat, through the blazing tropics, on ten days' rations of food.

I was in the islands to write letters for the weekly edition of the Sacramento 'Union,' a rich and influential daily journal which hadn't any use for them, but could afford to spend twenty dollars a week for nothing.

I had been in the islands several months when the survivors arrived. I was laid up in my room at the time, and unable to walk. Here was a great occasion to serve my journal, and I not able to take advantage of it. Necessarily I was in deep trouble. But by good luck his Excellency Anson Burlingame was there at the time, on his way to take up his post in China, where he did such good work for the United States. He came and put me on a stretcher and had me carried to the hospital where the shipwrecked men were, and I never needed to ask a question. He attended to all of that himself, and I had nothing to do but make the notes.

—*My Debut as a Literary Person,* 1903

The county campground along the river on the outskirts of Aitkin was cool under the new-growth shade trees. I pulled my canoe and bags onto a grassy ledge that overlooked the river, in sight of a single RV parked near the boat ramp, claiming its assigned parking slot. I liked the idea of not having an assigned place to camp. Just the idea made me feel a bit further out on the edge. I stowed my gear inside my tent, pulled the storm shelter over everything, dragged the canoe under a canopy of leaves at the edge of the woods and set out on the 20-minute walk into town.

The hamlet of Aitkin boasts 1,984 occupants and the

one-street strip of downtown was decorated in purple. There was purple everywhere I looked. Every storefront I walked past proclaimed in purple an annual event called Relay for Life. I grabbed a pizza at the town's only pizza joint and asked the proprietor about Relay for Life.

"What you've got is a town that is collectively fighting cancer," the man explained. He said he couldn't see such a thing happening in the big city in Florida that he had just moved from.

"How are they doing that?" I asked.

"They're getting it out into the open – the dreaded 'C' word. They're holding benefits and raising money, and there have been people here, old and young, who have then gone on to beat it."

I wrote down the names of the people he could think of and asked what time the diner across the street and the town's newspaper office a few doors down opened their doors in the morning. Both opened early.

That night my radar for a "positive American story" was at full alert. But over at the local tavern, the screen seemed to go blank for a time. Three locals were drinking heavily and they called me over to join in their revelry. The owner tended bar and knew everyone. I followed her lead and joined the three merrymakers. Like magic, my glass stein was refilled several times over, and then I was off, out onto the street, stumbling down the gravel road in search of my campsite.

One sure thing about paddling this river is that people will buy you drinks wherever you go. The more you try to pay, the more adamantly they refuse. People like to hear your stories and they like to tell you theirs. Their stories hadn't diluted my reservoir of good feeling, and as I laid my head down that night, I smiled, and then I was out.

Here in Aitkin, in Minnesota's Wild North, folks don't mess around when it comes to cancer. Come morning, I knew that I'd be in town for the entire day and I brought along all of my camera gear. It was already a sweltering day and it felt good to be on foot on a long, dusty road with a purpose and a story lead. I wore my Banana Republic "safari & travel" jacket for good luck. I introduced myself to the receptionist at the *Independent Age*, Aitkin's newspaper, and told her what I was up to. I had the on-the-road stubble of an itinerant scribe, a tripod and cameras – and a grin. I explained what a "citizen journalist" was – that it, in effect, meant that I was unqualified, unprofessional, and most certainly unpaid. Nevertheless, I did have a relationship with the producers at CNN and most of my stories were being used on the main page of CNN.com and occasionally on the air. Kathleen Pakarinen came out and shook my hand, asking how she could help. Within minutes, we had the co-chairwoman of the county's Relay for Life committee, Elaine Hill, in the office. I was given use of the paper's conference room, where I set up for my first interview of the day.

"We decided we would promote awareness," Elaine explained.

And they were most certainly doing it. In the week leading up to the town's big event, Aitkin was draped in purple, the designated color of the American Cancer Society. Shops were decorated in purple to celebrate survivors. Town folk drank purple smoothies. Money was raised from businesses and individuals. Everyone was committed to the cause. As I sat in a front booth at the Birchwood Café, reading the *Independent Age* and charging my array of electronic gear, the waitress hung streamers of twisted purple in the window as passers-by took immediate notice.

Relay for Life operates in association with the American Cancer Society and is billed as its signature fund-raising event. Elaine Hill had explained that the money collected "goes to research and to different services that are available, including free wigs, a feel-better program" for women and men and, when needed, "a free hospital bed."

But the story of fighting cancer in Aitkin runs deeper than affiliation with Relay for Life. In a town of this size, when somebody gets cancer, it's personal, because everybody knows the patient. In a single day I found myself inundated by stories of survival. As important as monetary support might be, the moral support lent by the town is perhaps more significant. "Even if it's just in one person's life, it's still a difference in their life and it's very important to them," said one young man whom I interviewed on the street. The survivor stories of Kathie Smith, 36, and Austin Price, 6, came to represent Aitkin's collective attitude.

Kathie is a mom of two young children who fought and beat colon cancer; her free-and-clear prognosis came back that very week. She explained how her former classmates and church and community friends had rallied together to throw a benefit to help cover her medical costs. "I was just in awe," she said. "I knew I was loved but I had no idea – how this community comes together when somebody is really financially strapped, emotionally, physically."

But it was the story of how Kathie's kids had dealt with her illness that had touched me, particularly her family's relationship with a little boy named Austin Price. His survival had taught her kids that getting cancer doesn't mean that you'll die.

"Austin Price," began Kathie, fighting back tears as she tried to tell a story that she still couldn't quite believe. "I graduated with his mom, Heidi. And we've been friends since about the third grade, so I've known Heidi for a very long time. And Austin and my kids went to day care together. And when he was diagnosed, he was about 4 1/2 years old and it was very hard on my kids – especially my son. He had a lot of questions about death and cancer and at that time he really believed that when you get cancer you die. And Austin proved that all wrong."

The interview with Austin and his family was one that I'll not soon forget. It began to rain as I walked up the hill, over the railroad tracks, just above the town's business district. I had spoken with the mother by phone. She had seemed apprehensive about speaking on camera but willing to meet and to say hello, if I could meet her and the kids at the house of a family friend that "was in a little better condition" than her own. The sun broke through the clouds as I knocked on the front door, holding a scrap of paper with the address in one hand and my tripod in the other. I could hear the laughter of boys, followed by shushes – and then the door opened.

Heidi was a working mother whose kind eyes brimmed with motherly love. As we spoke, her husband, Jason, drove up. Like his wife, he stood humbly, removing his ball cap and patting down his hair. He said with a smile that he wasn't going to speak on camera. He had just done some roofing or some similar work and felt that he wasn't presentable. I wanted to tell the story of this family's struggle – if they were willing to tell it. Theirs was the hesitancy of people who didn't seek the limelight.

I told them of my own mother, who was diagnosed with cancer when I was 10, and who had fought valiantly for the rest of my childhood. I told them of my best friend as a child – "Stan the Man," we called him – who had died of leukemia when we were both 12. The story of Stan's struggle with his disease had been reported in a local newspaper and it was an inspiration to many, including me. I told them that it was also their story – the story of Austin and his parents – and that their advice and words of comfort could inspire others to hope.

Heidi looked at Austin and asked, "What do you think, little man?" Austin flashed a big, toothless smile and they all agreed. We went to the back porch, where the sun had nearly dried the afternoon rain from a table and chairs. I set up my tripod and took out my cameras.

"His leg was a little bit swollen," Jason began, "and the doctors kept treating him for Lyme disease, thinking that that is what it was. They took him over to Brainerd – finally – and had them look at it over there and come to find out the doctor felt a lump. [They had] him sent to Children's Medical Center down in Minneapolis. From there they had felt a large mass – and the doctors kept him there."

"It was a tumor," Austin chimed in.

"It was a tumor," Jason continued. "So they had some scans and things – and they found four throughout his body. Two days later we were in full treatment."

Heidi continued the story as Austin examined my video camera, checking it out with a look of wonderment before going back to his mother's lap.

And then when I went up to bed she come up with me and fetched her candle, and tucked me in, and mothered me so good I felt mean, and like I couldn't look her in the face; and she set down on the bed and talked with me a long time, and said what a splendid boy Sid was, and didn't seem to want to ever stop talking about him; and kept asking me every now and then if I reckoned he could a got lost, or hurt, or maybe drownded, and might be laying at this minute somewheres suffering or dead, and she not by him to help him, and so the tears would drip down silent, and I would tell her that Sid was all right, and would be home in the morning, sure; and she would squeeze my hand, or maybe kiss me, and tell me to say it again, and keep on saying it, because it done her good, and she was in so much trouble.

—*Adventures of Huckleberry Finn*, 1884, Chapter 41

"We didn't get to go home. They just told us, 'You can't go home – it's too fast moving. We want you to start treatment on Saturday,'" Heidi said. "So Saturday morning he had a port put in and we started eight months of treatment."

Austin oohed and aahed over the number 8, looking up to his mother to make sure he was really in the hospital for that long. Jason and the family's youngest son, Nathan, looked on and smiled.

"We weren't home much for about four months," Heidi recalled. "Jason's mom and some friends did a benefit for his fifth birthday – cause he turned 5 a month after he was diagnosed. He turned 5 and they threw him a big birthday party. And he wants a party like that now every year… And then my sister and a few other people did one more benefit. This was supposed to be more of his birthday party but it did turn out to be a really good benefit. And the other one was strictly a benefit and I think it was very beneficial for him, too, because he just got to see so many people that he hadn't seen. There were so many kids. He was so excited to be somewhat normal for a day."

When I asked Austin what he wanted to say about his fight, what advice he might give, the 6-year-old spoke like a sage.

"Be strong," Austin said, rubbing his index finger against his forehead for further inspiration. "Be strong and be brave."

CHAPTER
THE WISDOM OF
WILDNESS
FOUR

In homage to the
Upper Mississippi River…

IT HAPPENED OFTEN. I'd be in a tavern, a cafe or a store, nowhere near my canoe or my gear. Somebody would take a look at me, tap the shoulder of a companion turn back to me and say: "You're doing the river. You're gonna go all the way, aren'tcha?"

I don't know what gives it away. I'd always leave my Muck Boots in my trusty Old Town canoe. Maybe it was the look in my eyes. Wanderlust. The state of being on an expedition, a safari – the state of being at one with nature while thoroughly enthralled by everyone and everything.

The next set of questions in northern Minnesota, from the very start, would come in the same sequence (and thus in order of importance), from fishermen, from children, from the odd, inquisitive observer, always with a smile:

1. "Are ya fishin'?"

2. "What'cha eatin'?"

3. "You're tentin' out, aren't'cha?"

I didn't always have a good answer for the first two questions, but I certainly did for the third. I had precious little backwoods experience when I set out on the river. But I found that "tentin' out" along the Upper Mississippi is a load of fun, and, yes, you drop the "g" if fittin' in is your aim. State-maintained, river-access-only campsites are placed strategically all along this portion of the river, complete with wooden benches and fire rings. A spectacular view of the river usually completes the package. Selecting the right tent is key. Your tent shelters you from mosquitoes, wind and rain, and protection from the elements proved to be very important because it rained nearly every night during my first month out. Some lightning strikes were so bright that, even with the rain fly draped over the tent, the inside lit up like it was high noon. It was like a charge of dynamite had gone off just outside the tent, and just as terrifying.

The storm come on again, after midnight. It got awful dark; the rain poured down; hail, too; the thunder boomed and roared and bellowed; the wind blowed a hurricane; and the lightning spread

78

over everything in big sheets of glare, and showed the whole raft as plain as day; and the river lashed up white as milk as far as you could see for miles, and there was that bar'l jiggering along, same as ever. The captain ordered the watch to man the after sweeps for a crossing, and nobody would go – no more sprained ankles for them, they said. They wouldn't even walk aft. Well then, just then the sky split wide open, with a crash, and the lightning killed two men of the after watch, and crippled two more. Crippled them how, says you? Why, sprained their ankles.

—*Life on the Mississippi,* 1883, Chapter 3

Despite the occasional, too-near lightning strike, you feel secure in your tent. It becomes your personal domain, your refuge. You can close yourself off from the world, or, by zipping open the screens and flaps, you can invite the world in. Sometimes it's the river rising to within a step or two of the front flap, sometimes leaden clouds grumbling in the distance, sometimes fistsful of lightning hurled down, it seems, by an angry god. You get giddy becoming so intimate with the earth and the sky.

Getting back onto the river is a cause for celebration, akin to a cleansing of body, mind and soul, something that feels good and wholesome and right. The freedom from meetings, clocks and calendars was finally sinking in. *I was on the river.* It's hard to describe – that feeling of peace, that inner feeling of pure tranquility. But it was there for that moment, and it was there plenty strong. No doubt others have felt it as well.

> *I never felt easy till the raft was two mile below there and out in the middle of the Mississippi. Then we hung up our signal lantern, and judged that we was free and safe once more. I hadn't had a bite to eat since yesterday, so Jim he got out some corn-dodgers and buttermilk, and pork and cabbage and greens — there ain't nothing in the world so good when it's cooked right — and whilst I eat my supper we talked and had a good time. I was powerful glad to get away from the feuds, and so was Jim to get away from the swamp. We said there warn't no home like a raft, after all. Other places do seem so cramped up and smothery, but a raft don't. You feel mighty free and easy and comfortable on a raft.*

—*Adventures of Huckleberry Finn*, 1884, Chapter 18

There's a connection to this river that's impossible to explain unless you've ridden upon it at length, lived alongside it or opened yourself up to it. It's a sort of love affair that began to develop at this stage of my journey. The river was starting to talk to me, to whisper sweet nothings, to tell me her stories. I was an obliging and eager audience.

The early sun peeks through translucent clouds or the tops of bankside trees, conjuring flickering shapes on the water. The river reflects the leaves, dancing in a cool breeze, on either side of its still-narrow course. But then the sun comes out in full force, stunningly bright and omnipresent. I paddled throughout the day, zipping off the bottoms of my convertible trousers to create shorts, taking off all superfluous clothing, alternating between paddling hard and taking it easy, at least when the current cooperated.

Once a day, with the canoe drifting sideways in a steady, gentle, downriver current, I laid back, struck a match to light an American Spirit cigarette and enjoyed a smoke. With my bare feet on the canoe's yoke, taking in the immense heavens and the clouds drifting overhead, I paid homage to Huckleberry Finn.

> *I got out amongst the driftwood, and then laid down in the bottom of the canoe and let her float. I laid there, and had a good rest and a smoke out of my pipe, looking away into the sky; not a cloud in it. The sky looks ever so deep when you lay down on your back in the moonshine; I never knowed it before.*

—Adventures of Huckleberry Finn, 1884, Chapter 7

A stylized image of an eagle is printed on the paper of each cigarette. And, as I inhaled and exhaled, on one day in particular, I noticed a bald eagle perched in a tree, just up and to my side, silently surveying the same vista of this glorious land, but from a more majestic vantage point. Or was it?

I try to explain to people, and to remember it correctly myself, that there is nothing quite like being on the water, down low in a canoe, effortlessly gliding along. It is unadulterated bliss. It liberates the mind from everyday worries and cares. The river gently sweeps you into a union with nature. You watch with a sense of wonder as fish dart this way and that beside the canoe, as deer and painted turtles, beavers and foxes and waterfowl of all varieties and hues appear along the banks. Beneath the canoe, strands of water grass and the reeds along the shore point in the direction of the river's flow. And overhead, the clouds and the sun, the moon and the stars hold sway in an ever-changing sky.

Lacking human contact, I began to whistle with the birds, and they whistled back. Well, to be honest, only loons engage in repartee, and maybe only with loonies like me. You encounter loons at the outset on the Upper Mississippi. It's always a delight because when you whistle, they answer back, as if to challenge you to justify your opinions. You find them in small groups, in pairs, or on their own. In Minnesota's Wild North, loons are easily identified by their black heads and black-and-white plumage. They dive and stay underwater for long spells and rarely let you get close, save for one loon who wet his whistle to call again and again. He might have been running for office, but I never did find out.

Tree swallows swarmed along the river at times, heeding a mysterious impulse to change direction simultaneously in a split second, the sunlight momentarily catching the undersides of their iridescent, blue-green wings. I liked to think they were celebrating my voyage. But when I got my mind out of the clouds and took a closer look, I saw that their juking and jiving was more than a celebratory show in my honor. The swallows were actually in pursuit of dragonflies, bees and wasps. Once, a tree swallow swooped down right in front of me, inches from my nose, and expertly grasped an unsuspecting dragonfly in its flight across the river. It all happened so fast that all I could do was utter "Wow!"

It was along this stretch of the river that I set my record for the most miles paddled in a single day: 58. The feat occurred between the Willow Wood campsite and the town of Palisade, Minn. I had heard good things about the town from two separate fishermen, specifically about the Palisade Café. Always a sucker for a greasy spoon, I paddled toward the town with all the strength I could muster. But by the time I arrived at the last campsite before Palisade, I was still 15 miles shy of the town. It was only 7:30 p.m. with plenty of daylight remaining. I rounded a bend and looked toward the lonely campsite on my left. I didn't want to land just yet. The site looked deserted and devoid of life, save for mosquitoes, as well as cold and damp because of the low-hanging branches that sheltered it. Out on the river there were no mosquitoes and there was far too much daylight left to settle for such a campsite.

Life is like that. The older I get the more I realize that Joseph Heller had it right – life is full of Catch-22s. Fifteen river miles equated to about 4 ½ hours of paddling. So if I stayed at the campsite, I'd miss breakfast the next morning in Palisade, unless of course I departed before first light. And if I pressed on, it would be dark before I got to Palisade that night.

I pulled out my map and saw that Wold's Ferry Crossing was five miles downriver. If I played my cards right, I'd arrive at sunset, which at that time of year was about 9 p.m. The only problem was that Wold's Ferry Crossing wasn't a campsite; it was a boat landing. I'd seen plenty of them by this time. Some might offer a grassy spot to pitch a tent, but camping at boat landings is usually illegal, and if a law officer turned up I'd have some explaining to do. I made a brash decision to keep on paddling and break the law. I'd shoot for Wold's Ferry Crossing and stay there, but I'd break camp at sunrise and head on down to Palisade for a hot country breakfast.

At 9 p.m. the sun was dipping behind the trees on the western bank of the river. Just then I saw people for the first time in several days. Two teenage boys were fishing from a flat-bottomed boat just off the boat ramp, shining lights into the water to attract fish. I said hello, pulled out my canoe at the landing and eyed the embankment. It offered a perfect patch of grass just up and to the side of the ramp. But a gigantic sign, erected by the great state of Minnesota, lorded over the grass. It proclaimed that camping at the spot was illegal. It cited code this and paragraph that and said that anyone who dared to camp at the site would be prosecuted and persecuted. Well, maybe the persecution was implied. But it was enough to send me on my way.

From the moment the sun goes down, you've got about an hour of twilight remaining. The sun's "after glow," I've heard it called. It's a lovely term, but when that last bit of illumination from the sun can mean your salvation, it takes on a more portentous meaning. I looked at my watch and again at the map. I figured that if I threw my better judgment to the wind, I'd have an hour to paddle in the after glow, followed by two hours of pitch darkness before I reached Palisade – if I reached Palisade.

I waved goodbye to the boys and laughed as I pitched back into the current. This stretch of the river is about as wide as a four-lane street, complete with sidewalks. Except for those boys, there was no river traffic to worry about. The danger here is the boulders that jut out into the river on either side, looking to capsize an unsuspecting canoeist pressing along in the dark.

As the last remnants of light faded away, I discovered a sense that I hardly knew I possessed and hadn't had much chance to use: night vision. I leaned forward, grabbed a lantern from one of my bags and put it on top of the foremost canvas duffle. I draped my French Foreign Legion hat over the lantern so that it blocked the light in my direction and reflected it forward.

There was a canopy of clouds, but a sliver of the moon occasionally pushed through. When the clouds parted, a glimmer of starlight provided a faint notion of my surroundings. I noticed that the tree line on either side of the river was only a fraction of a shade darker than the sky behind them. So I used the tree lines to guide my way. I refrained from paddling and ran with the current, not very fast, but certainly not too slow. My sense of hearing seemed to become more acute as I listened for rushing water, a sign of boulders ahead.

At this stage of the river, a canoeist encounters shallow water rushing over a bed of small rocks, forming Class 1 rapids. They're not scary. In fact, they're delightful, because they ripple and bubble and form a jet stream that propels the canoe forward. Your paddle is needed only to guide the canoe through the narrow channels or to push it off a sandbar. The cool night air rushed past and I grinned in the dark, as if I were a kid again on a swing, relishing that last downward and upward arc before Mom hollers that it's dinnertime. On the playground, a bully might grab the swing's chain and send you flying. Here, on the river, a boulder looming in the dark could do the same. But the consequences could be deadly.

At that point, I knelt down in my canoe, in the middle of the Mississippi River, and said a prayer. The next day would be Sunday, and it struck me as funny that I was paddling that night into the new week. I hadn't uttered a prayer in a long time, and I felt like a hypocrite praying because I was in danger. I felt sorry that I wasn't a stronger person, that I most certainly wasn't a saint. It was then that I made a promise to God, maybe because there was nobody else to talk to or maybe because I was right to be concerned about my safety. Clasping my hands and bowing my head, I said with conviction: "If I make it to Palisade alive, I'll go to church. I promise you that. I'll go to church." Mine was a faith of convenience.

> *"There never was anything like it. Now you may believe it or not, but as sure as I am sitting here, he brought my boat a-tilting down through those awful snags at Chicot under a rattling head of steam, and the wind a-blowing like the very nation, at that! My officers will tell you so. They saw it. And, sir, while he was a-tearing right down through those snags, and I a-shaking in my shoes and praying, I wish I may never speak again if he didn't pucker up his mouth and go to WHISTLING! Yes, sir; whistling "Buffalo gals, can't you come out tonight, can't you come out to-night, can't you come out to-night;" and doing it as calmly as if we were attending a funeral and weren't related to the corpse. And when I remonstrated with him about it, he smiled down on me as if I was his child, and told me to run in the house and try to be good, and not be meddling with my superiors!"*

—*Life on the Mississippi*, 1883, Chapter 14

During that fearful night on the Mississippi, banks of clouds sometimes obliterated any ambient light from the moon and stars. Along one stretch, as my canoe rode the current in inky blackness, the river took a hard turn to the right and then, doubling back on itself, veered sharply to the left. On the bank just above this horseshoe bend, I saw a house decked out in lights. It was a modern log house with big windows and natural beams. The lights illuminated its riverfront yard, prime real estate because of the picturesque location.

I heard voices and the squeals of children. I peered ahead and saw the silhouettes of a trio of kids along the river's edge, waving flashlights wildly about. They called out to me but I couldn't understand what they said. I continued to paddle for all I was worth and tried to navigate the sharp bend, using my own flashlight to look out for overhanging tree limbs. The children called out again, but I couldn't hear them over the rushing water. "What did you say?" I shouted. "Say again. I couldn't hear you!" Craning my neck to listen, I made out their faint query: "Are they biting?"

"No. I'm not fishing. I'm canoeing!" I shouted back, to which one of the kids yelled, hesitantly, "Oh, OK!" They ran back into the house, and then a man came out with a lantern. He aimed the light in my direction, probably wondering if I posed a danger to his family. He didn't say a word, but I knew instinctively what he was thinking. During daylight hours, I was a friend to one and all, someone worthy of a friendly greeting or a cheerful wave. But in the dark, I was an object of fear. Only someone running from the law, people probably thought, would be in a canoe on the river at such an hour. Only somebody desperate, or maybe somebody not quite real, a specter, would be on the river on a pitch-black night.

I hunched over my seat, dipped my paddle into the water and propelled myself forward into the darkness. The way one of the kids shouted "Oh, OK!" with a hint of apprehension was a sign of fright. I thought with some amusement that I may have launched a family legend that night, about the time in July 2009 when a ghost floated by the house in the dead of night.

Such a catastrophe would be death, in all probability, for we would be swept to sea in the "Sink" or overturned and drowned. We warned Ollendorff to keep his wits about him and handle himself carefully, but it was useless; the moment the bow touched the bank, he made a sprin and the canoe whirled upside down in ten-foot water.

—*Roughing It*, 1872, Chapter 31

What brought those folks out that night was a break in the weather. It was a hot night, the first in about a month that didn't bring rain. Families ventured out that night to light bonfires, roast marshmallows, play games and tell tales. I could smell the wood smoke and the burning marshmallows, and my stomach ached with hunger. Throughout that evening, people would leave their bonfires, gather at the water's edge, peer out at the river by lantern light, seldom saying a word, and follow my passage along their portion of the river.

I didn't say a word, either, and concentrated my full attention on the river ahead. It might sound funny, but a sense of calm and security descended upon me that night, a feeling that I would make it to the end. I heard the burbling of fast water before I came to it. I found the boulders with my flashlight in time to avoid smashing into them. I saw in time the low tree branches that might have knocked me from the canoe.

Then, at last, came the bridge. I had been focusing so intently on potential hazards that I lost track of time. And here I was at Palisade. The bridge marked the town and, over to the right, the little park, where I dragged my canoe and gear out of the water and onto the grass. I swiftly made camp and crawled into my tent. My muscles were sore and my back was thankful for a rest. It was midnight, and I had been paddling for 17 hours straight.

On the walk into Palisade the next morning, the sun was bright and the townspeople were out and about. Some passed me on their John Deeres and tipped their caps. A sign proclaimed, "Palisade, Population 109." I found the greasy spoon, but before that, the town's only church. A sign out front said the service would start at 9:30. I looked at my watch, which said 9:28. "OK, I'll do it," I said to myself – and God. "But let me plug in my laptop first." So I walked over to the Palisade Café and asked if I could charge my laptop while I went to church. I promised to return and order the manliest breakfast on the menu. The waitresses smiled and waved, and one said to another, "Oh, ain't that sweet! The young man's goin' on over to church."

At the church steps, I took off my cap, grabbed a bottle of water from my bag and poured some of it on my head, just enough to pat down my disheveled hair to make me look respectable – and reverent.

I pulled open the big wooden door and stepped inside. I signed the guest registry and wrote down my address: "The Mississippi River." I was late, but I knew it didn't matter. I took a seat in the back pew and smiled. The sun shone brightly through the stained-glass windows on a congregation mostly of farming families in their Sunday best. One lady stood to deliver a report on a community center that was filling to the brim with donated goods for the poor. Then came a hymn, one whose words I didn't know. It was called "Great is Thy Faithfulness." We stood to sing, and as I read the words in the hymnal, I found my own voice making "a joyful noise unto the Lord."

Summer and winter and springtime and harvest,

The sun, the moon, and stars in their courses above.

Join with all nature in manifold witness

To Thy great faithfulness, mercy and love.

Great is Thy faithfulness! Great is Thy faithfulness!

I was glad I kept my promise.

CHAPTER

THE SOMALI-AMERICAN

JOURNEY

FIVE

*Somali-American sisters,
Minneapolis, Minn.*

THE WORD *SAFARI* EVOKES IMAGES of African savannahs and exotic wildlife like cheetahs, rhinos and lions, or perhaps Henry Morton Stanley's search for Dr. Livingston. We might imagine a safari as a vacation for the very rich, not an excursion likely to be undertaken by average folks along the Mississippi River.

But the word *safari* in Swahili, the *lingua franca* of East Africa, simply means "long journey." It comes originally from the Arabic word *safra,* which also means "journey." But the journeys referred to by that word were those by Bedouins and their camels across vast expanses of desert in Arabia and the Horn of Africa.

The 20th-century adventurer Sir Wilfred Thesiger, who was born in Abyssinia, now called Ethiopia, wrote of a lifetime of travel in such books as *Arabian Sands* and *The Marsh Arabs*. For Thesiger, a safari wasn't a trip for the wealthy or elite. "Once an old man in rags joined us," Thesiger wrote in *Arabian Sands*. "My companions, some thirty of them (for we were traveling through hostile country), greeted him with great respect. I asked the youngest why they paid him so much deference. 'Because he is generous. He hasn't now, but once he owned many camels; he killed them all to feed his guests, till at last he had none left.' I could hear the respect, even envy in the boy's voice."

The late photojournalist Dan Eldon, a fellow admirer of Thesiger, underlined the following passage in his tattered copy of *Arabian Sands*: "I have often looked back into my childhood for a clue to this perverse necessity which drives me from my own land to the deserts of the East." Dan lost his life in 1993 at age 22 in that desert region of East Africa. He was stoned to death by a mob, along with three other journalists in Mogadishu, Somalia, while working as a photographer for Reuters news agency. But the story of Dan Eldon is a celebration of life, of a life well lived, of a life that continues to touch and inspire many. He valued such traits as "energy, sincerity, clarity of vision and creativity," and he incorporated them into a mission statement for his existence on this planet. He called it "Safari as a way of life."

Mark Twain, known best as a Mississippi River steamboat pilot who became an author, also knew a thing or two about safaris outside his native America. And his interest, like that of Thesiger and Eldon, was mostly in the people.

We wanted something thoroughly and uncompromisingly foreign – foreign from top to bottom – foreign from center to circumference – foreign inside and outside and all around – nothing anywhere about it to dilute its foreignness – nothing to remind us of any other people or any other land under the sun. And lo! In Tangier we have found it. Here is not the slightest thin that ever we have seen save in pictures – and we always mistrusted the pictures before. We cannot anymore. The pictures used to seem exaggerations – they seemed too weird and fanciful for reality. But behold, they were not wild enough – they were not fanciful enough – they have not told half the story. Tangier is a foreign land if ever there was one, and the true spirit of it can never be found in any book save The Arabian Nights. Here are no white men visible, yet swarms of humanity are all about us...

There are stalwart Bedouins of the desert here, and stately Moors proud of a history that goes back to the night of time; and Jews whose fathers fled hither centuries upon centuries ago; and swarthy Riffians from the mountains – born cut-throats – and original, genuine Negroes as black as Moses; and howling dervishes and a hundred breeds of Arabs—all sorts and descriptions of people that are foreign and curious to look upon.

—*The Innocents Abroad*, 1869, Chapter 8

You do not read *The Journey is the Destination: The Journals of Dan Eldon;* you experience it. For me, the acquaintance was made in the late 1990s, and the message resonated. Through his journal and collages, which include photographs, pen-and-ink drawings, feathers, blood and beads, I felt that I knew Dan, although I never met him in person. As a youth, I attended a Rudolf Steiner School, emphasizing art and music, as Dan did; I was living in Africa in 1993 when Dan was killed; and many of my experiences were similar to Dan's. I've had rocks hurled at me in a South African township, I've witnessed an attempted coup d'état, and I've had a long love affair with Africa, its resilient people and its rich, red soil. I feel like I know Dan, like I've been on safari with him.

I was recalling the high and low points of our respective journeys through life as I paddled toward Minnesota's Twin Cities, Minneapolis-St. Paul, and a random factoid floated through my brain: Minneapolis has the highest percentage of Somali refugees in the United States.

That's it! My story for Minneapolis would delve into the Somali-American community with, I hoped, a positive spin. The day suddenly brimmed with possibilities. I pulled my canoe out of the river and into the shade of a medley of maple and sycamore trees, got out my cellphone and rang up Kat Fowler, a producer with the Eldon family's Creative Visions Foundation in Malibu, Calif. We had been in communication when I was planning my Mississippi River trip, and Dan's mother, Kathy, had been supportive and inspirational. I knew that she or her staff would have a suggestion for a solid lead on the Somalis in Minneapolis, and, sure enough, I was given the name of a Muslim-American community organizer in the city: Farheen Hakeem.

When I got to Minneapolis, I contacted Ms. Hakeem and then did a little research on her. She had been a Green Party candidate for mayor, an educator, a Muslim-American community leader and organizer, and a volunteer, spending a good portion of her time with Somali-American Girl Scouts in the Cedar-Riverside area of Minneapolis, called "Little Mogadishu."

Ms. Hakeem and her Girl Scouts were no strangers to the media. They had been featured on the front page of *The New York Times* on Nov. 28, 2007, and in the documentary *Bismillah*, which won a College Emmy in 2008. A copy of the documentary, produced and directed by Jolene Pinder and Sarah Zaman, was made available to me, and after watching the film I phoned Pinder to get her take on the effect Ms. Hakeem was having on the girls she was serving.

"Farheen is empowering a new generation of girls," Pinder gushed over the phone from New York. "She's an amazing role model … shaping how the girls see their role in the community – the power and voice they can have."

There was no question that this woman was making an impact, and I was eager to meet her. We agreed to meet at the Wilde Roast Café in the artsy Nordeast neighborhood. I had scouted out the place and chose it partly because its sidewalk wicker chairs were reminiscent of old Constantinople.

Ms. Hakeem arrived, smiling broadly and wearing a black *hijab*. We took seats in the sunshine, each with a camera to capture the moment. We sipped *café au laits* and laughed at the cameras that we both tried our best to ignore.

"Well, part of being a Muslim-American girl [is] part of the challenges of just being a girl in general," she explained. "You know, you're sitting there thinking, 'Am I good enough, am I smart enough, am I pretty enough, am I skinny enough?' and the challenges that girls face with that. On top of that, being Muslim, where you're also being told you're not supposed to care about any of that stuff, you know, 'cause you're teaching girls that modesty is more important, because it's who you are inside that matters more than who you are outside."

The journey of these girls was different from the one that brought their parents from Somalia. Theirs was a journey bridging the divide between the Old Country and the New. I wanted to learn about their future, about their next steps in becoming integrated into their new country and becoming Americans.

"So those are the challenges," Ms. Hakeem continued. "It's this double whammy, I think, with … Muslim-American girls. As they define their place: 'I'm American – this is who I am, this is part of who I am.' And then they're dealing with the challenges of being a girl, saying: 'I can study whatever I want, I can do whatever I want, there is nothing that can stop me from being a president or being a doctor or a lawyer or a senator, or whatever it may be.' When you have both of those challenges that are there, you see these girls persevere and become extremely strong and it's quite remarkable to see that – to see them grow that way."

Ms. Hakeem smiled broadly as she spoke of her Girl Scouts, one of whom she had recently adopted. She radiated joy as she described each girl in detail, each trial and tribulation, each hope and aspiration, each building block toward fostering creativity, courage and success. She wasn't praising herself; she was lavishing praise on the girls. Although she was an inspiration, it was clear that the girls were making their own decisions, were the masters of their own destiny.

I was able to shadow for a day two of the girls featured in the film *Bismillah*. Mary Metchnnek, a Christian, 15, and Ayan Deria, a Muslim Somali-American, 16, are best friends. Together, we toured "Little Mogadishu" in the Cedar-Riverside community near downtown Minneapolis.

Starting from the Brian Coyle Center at the University of Minnesota, where Somali children tapped on computer keyboards, talked music, and shot baskets, we went to an inner-city landmark, Cedar-Riverside Plazas, a high-rise complex of low-income housing. It is easy to be swayed into a belief that a place is good or bad, depending on whom you talk to or to what idle chatter you might be privy to. I had been told how dangerous this area was, how full of drugs, how gang-infested, how deplorable and degenerate were the people who lived here. And yet here I was, walking through one of the main buildings with its residents, witnessing a reversal of what I had previously been led to believe. At "E" building of Cedar-Riverside Plazas, near the Brian Coyle Center, I saw parks, swimming pools and a computer lab, all in use, filled with kids who appeared confident, comfortable – even fearless.

"You used to not be able to enter that area," Ms. Hakeem said. "But now you can walk around freely, even at 10 p.m. at night." When I asked how the change came about, she said that the "elders" of the Somali community would sit outdoors late into the night, keeping vigil over their Cedar-Riverside neighborhood, ready to set straight any wayward youths. "When the Somali refugees began to arrive," Ms. Hakeem continued, "they naturally moved into the least expensive section of town – Cedar-Riverside. They, in fact, succeeded in turning it around."

As I entered the neighborhood to meet Ms. Hakeem and the girls, my 25-year-old taxi driver, Hassan Mohamed, gave his take on the turnabout. "We get along in America," he said, referring to his fellow Somalis. "When we came to America we are very helpful to each other and other people, too... Back in Somalia it's all about tribes, and every tribe wants to be the president. But here we put the tribes to the side – to come together."

[N]ow and then his mind reverted to his treatment by those rude Christ's Hospital boys, and he said, "When I am king, they shall not have bread and shelter only, but also teachings out of books; for a full belly is little worth where the mind is starved, and the heart. I will keep this diligently in my remembrance, that this day's lesson be not lost upon me, and my people suffer thereby; for learning softeneth the heart and breedeth gentleness and charity."

—*The Prince and the Pauper,* 1882, Chapter 4

Part of learning about pride in a community comes from pitching in to help it out. As we walked along the streets and under the bridges from Cedar-Riverside to the area called Seward, best friends Ayan and Mary flinched at the sight of police vehicles racing past, blue lights flashing and sirens blaring. "The cops here don't really care for us – for anybody of color," Ayan said. The mood of the afternoon turned a bit sour with the sight of the police cars and the girl's remark, but it brightened again when we arrived at the girls' latest community project, a mural of Minneapolis sponsored by ArtiCulture.

Elizabeth Greenbaum, executive director of ArtiCulture,

a nonprofit arts education center, called art "a wonderful equalizer, especially for students who don't succeed in other subject matters."

"When you think about it and take it a step further," she said, "we're talking about the basic understanding and the basic concepts to write – and that leads into reading and that leads into learning – so [the] arts are very much orientated to learning on all levels."

Asked what the mural meant to her personally, Ayan grinned and said, "I think it's trying to say what the community is about. Like little parts of it. Like the river and downtown area. That everything is part of the community." The girl was busily working on the mural, painting red beads on the head of a little girl wearing a shirt with a happy face, hand in hand with a mother in a *hijab*.

I looked around and tried to put this mural and what it represented – this new concept of "community" – into context, to find out what it meant to the neighbors, to see if they approved. Adjacent to the ArtiCulture offices on East Franklin Avenue is Jim's Barber Shop, which Jim and his father have manned for the past 50 years. I asked Jim what he thought about the mural, on one side of the building that houses his shop. "I think it's a great idea," he said. "I'm very impressed with the groups of people who go there." Asked how the older people, mostly of German and Swedish extraction, are adapting to the influx of Somali refugees, Jim thought for a moment before replying: "While most people are OK with it, overall I think a lot of the seniors aren't adapting." He was quick to point out, however, that most of these same old-timers had once been immigrants themselves.

A part of any journey is looking back. Such was the case with Somali immigrant and political refugee Safia Wardere, who came to America with her husband in 1993 because their country was at war. The woman, dressed in a traditional purple *khimar*, a headscarf that hangs down to just above the waist, spoke broken English as I interviewed her. She was a proud woman who exhibited a fine wit in both English and Somali, laughed easily, and displayed a deep love for her 13-year-old daughter, Shachi Hussin.

I asked Shachi how she views her life in America and about her hopes in this country. "My life was hard, because I had to keep my tradition – but still try to fit in with the American culture," she said with a smile, shaking her head from side to side under the white shawl of her *hijab*. "And in my future what I hope is to become a doctor, to help people."

For the next generation of Somali-Americans, like Shachi, the task is twofold: to keep one foot planted in the here and now, the "now" shaped by the past, and the other in an American future that is both promising and unpredictable.

I wanted to make a connection in my mind between the Somali refugees in Minneapolis and the conditions in Somalia that precipitated their move to America. So I asked Dan Eldon biographer Jennifer New and Kathy Eldon about Dan's work in Somalia in the 1990s. That was at the onset of a Somali drought that resulted in famine and escalation of that most ironic of conflicts, a "civil" war.

All war must be just the killing of strangers against whom you feel no personal animosity; strangers whom, in other circumstances, you would help if you found them in trouble, and who would help you if you needed it.

—*The Private History of the Campaign That Failed,* 1885

"Dan had a beer with his friend Aidan Hartley," said Jennifer New, author of *Dan Eldon: The Art of Life,* referring to another journalist based in Nairobi, Kenya. "Aidan told him a little of what was happening in Somalia and invited him to come along on his next trip north."

"In 1991, Dan took his camera into southern Somalia, where he heard that there was a famine raging in the region around Bidoah," Kathy Eldon said, picking up the story.

Dan and Aidan reported on the famine, and their photos and stories were picked up by *The Nation* newspaper of Nairobi and by Reuters news agency. Their reports on the terrible famine unfolding in Somalia were disseminated around the world. The experience was horrifying for Dan because, until he had gone to Somalia, he had never seen a person die. But there, in that impoverished desert nation in the Horn of Africa, he had witnessed women, children and the elderly dying by the hundreds.

"Dan's stories and images and Aidan's stories helped launch a global response that led to Operation Restore Hope, which brought the much-needed aid into southern Somalia," Kathy Eldon said. "Dan returned again and again, over the next year, to try to tell the story to a world community. Frustrated when they weren't paying attention; thrilled when they did pay attention, [when they did] something.

"However, the situation grew steadily worse," she went on. "Dan was called to the scene of a terrible bombing by U.N. forces of a house where they believed the warlord Gen. [Mohamed Farrah] Aidid was hiding. As it happened, the warlord was not there and the troops bombed the house anyway and more than 50 children and women and men were killed and over 200 people were terribly wounded.

"Dan and three other colleagues came to the compound where the tragedy had happened and started shooting what was going on, but the people were so enraged by the sight of these foreigners, although two were Africans – they were Kenyans, Anthony Macharia, and Hos Mania. They picked up stones and sticks and they beat and shot the journalists to death. Dan was 22 years old when this happened."

Photojournalists like Dan Eldon and others who give their lives are important not only because their reporting sometimes leads to actions that alleviate suffering but also because they serve as inspiration for aspiring young journalists like Ruqiya and Muhuba – members of a new generation of

Somali-Americans who know about Somalia only through their parents and news stories.

I found Ruqiya and Muhuba, both 13, honing their skills at the Minnesota International Middle School, a private school that caters to the Somali-American community.

When girlfriends Ruqiya and Muhuba talk journalism at the school, they do so with a glint of passion that might be mistaken for surprise at finding themselves involved in such an enterprise. The two were part of a seven-student summer school journalism program, and they are starting to find their voices. Coming as they do from a community of refugees, they encounter negative press about their Muslim-American community as well as about Somalia, haunted by a civil war that has raged their entire lives.

"When I started researching things," Muhuba said, "I felt something that I've never felt before – I knew people were struggling ... It made me research more to know more."

Mark Twain marveled at progressive endeavors similar to that at the Minnesota International Middle School when he visited Minneapolis in 1882.

> *Sixteen railroads meet in Minneapolis, and sixty-five passenger trains arrive and depart daily. In this place, as in St. Paul, journalism thrives. Here there are three great dailies, ten weeklies, and three monthlies.*

> *There is a university, with four hundred students – and, better still,*

its good efforts are not confined to enlightening the one sex.

—*Life on the Mississippi,* 1883, Chapter 60

The legacy of Dan Eldon echoed in the remarks of Ruqiya and Muhuba, adolescent girls whose words were grandmotherly wise and youthfully idealistic.

"I learned that when you're a journalist, you get to save people's lives," Ruqiya said. "Not physically, but emotionally." There are "people in the shadows that people don't know about," she said, and it's important to help them.

Somali-born photographer Abdi Roble, like Dan Eldon, is an inspiration to the girls. His documentation of the Somali diaspora and humanitarian work prompted the school's administrator, Abdirashid Warsame, to return to Africa to see how he could help. Somali refugee camps are sprawled throughout Kenya and other parts of Africa, Warsame said. Only the lucky ones make it to America.

Ruqiya and Muhuba represent the next generation of U.S.-educated Somali-American journalists, just as many of the other Somali-American girls I interviewed for this story represent the future of law, politics and medicine in their community. Although barely adolescents, Ruqiya and Muhuba, have already interviewed the president of Puntland, a region of northeastern Somalia that became an autonomous state in 1998.

The president, Abdirahman Mohamed Mohamud, paid

a visit to their class the previous summer. "We weren't even expecting him," Muhuba said. "It was a surprise for us."

The president asked members of the class if they planned to return to Somalia. The girls beamed as they repeated the question put by the visiting official and answered in unison: "Yes, we do want to go back to Somalia… We want to make a difference."

CHAPTER

RETHINKING THE
AMERICAN FAMILY FARM

SIX

Cowboy Jeff Mueller with trademark cavalry hat, McGregor, Iowa

WHEN SIXTH-GENERATION cattle rancher Greg Koether helped pull my canoe out of the Mississippi at McGregor, Iowa, I had to smile. I had been on the river for more than a month at this point and was well downstream of the border between Minnesota and Iowa. The river was introducing me to a number of firsts in my life: the first time I'd united the words *canoe* and *expedition*; the first time I'd attended a Native-American powwow; the first time I'd explore and report on the very essence of the Heartland, a real American farm.

Anticipating the story, I imagined hearty, early-morning breakfasts; getting my hands dirty working the fields and tending the livestock; and sitting on the farmhouse porch in the evenings, listening to the crickets and engaging in thoughtful discussions about the triumphs and challenges of running a family farm. I was intent on getting the nitty-gritty of life on an all-American farm, finding out how it operated in the past, how it worked now and how it would be done decades down the road.

I wanted to focus on "sustainable agriculture." But at that time I hadn't the foggiest notion of what sustainable agriculture looked like up close or what the term actually means. I was steered to the Practical Farmers of Iowa, which, according to its website, promotes "profitable, ecologically sound, and community-enhancing approaches to agriculture through farmer-led investigation and information sharing."

PFI seems to have gotten the political balance about right. It's endorsed by both the conservative American Farm Bureau as well as Farm Aid, which has benefited from the singing talents of Willie Nelson and Neil Young.

The organization suggested that I cover a "farminar," a sort of field-day seminar on farming, which was to take place "just off the river." The Practical Farmers of Iowa, to which the Koether family belongs, is a modern-day farmers' cooperative that aims in part to combat the growing use of chemicals, farming by big corporations and the disintegration of farm

communities. I eagerly accepted the invitation, and the Koethers
were expecting my arrival. I hoped to learn about such things as
the true cost of "cheap" food and how sustainable agriculture
creates sustainable communities.

*In the course of the tug-boat gossip, it came out that out of every five
of my former friends who had quitted the river, four had chosen
farming as an occupation. Of course this was not because they
were peculiarly gifted, agriculturally, and thus more likely to succeed
as farmers than in other industries: the reason for their choice
must be traced to some other source. Doubtless they chose farming
because that life is private and secluded from irruptions of undesirable
strangers – like the pilot-house hermitage. And doubtless they also
chose it because on a thousand nights of black storm and danger they
had noted the twinkling lights of solitary farm-houses, as the boat
swung by, and pictured to themselves the serenity and security and
coziness of such refuges at such times, and so had by-and-bye come
to dream of that retired and peaceful life as the one desirable thing
to long for, anticipate, earn, and at last enjoy.*

—*Life on the Mississippi*, 1883, Chapter 49

As Greg Koether and I rolled along U.S. 18, my education
began. Greg was a real-deal farmer in every respect – everything
I hoped that the all-American farmer would be. He sported
a moustache, wore a blue silk scarf at his neck, spoke in a deep
voice with a hearty laugh always at he ready and possessed
a pair of gnarled, grandfatherly hands that told of a life of

hard work on the farm. When he shook my hand, his grip and his smile told me that I was welcome. I knew that if we stepped into a bar, he'd know the whole lot and that if fists and bottles started to fly, I'd be protected. There was nothing phony about him, about his one-ton Chevy flat-bed truck, or the place where we were headed.

I looked back onto the bed of the truck and then up to the tines of the bale unroller that held down my canoe and Duluth river bag, and then back to Greg. He had read my thoughts.

"It's alright," he said. "It'll hold just fine."

He was right. My canoe and bag were secure. And I was secure. In fact, I felt about as secure as I'd ever felt. The truck, the highway and the fields on either side were about as American as you could get. Here I was in the American Heartland and I was about to see it from a perspective I had never before considered. I trusted Greg and I think he could sense that, for what he said next amounted to a mission statement for the ideal, sustainable life.

"The return to Mother Nature's system – when you think about the number of years that she's been developing it – is going to be the healthiest solution to the world's ailments in every aspect that you can think of," he said. "It would lead to a healthy environment, healthy bank accounts, healthy people, and a healthy water supply – as simple as that, returning to what Mother Nature had long ago established."

Greg was resting his arm on the steering wheel, alternately

glancing out over the land and looking at me. "And I believe also," he went on, "that even though the population has multiplied many times over, employment and hunger would be greatly alleviated."

The words struck me like the Scout motto of my childhood: "Be prepared." The underlying message was something to live by, to aspire to. You could listen or not, but if you don't, don't say that you were never warned.

I glanced at Greg and saw that he was looking forward, hand on the wheel, surveying the land while thinking hard about life and how the future might play out. He wasn't someone who passively watches from the sidelines. He was a doer, and his philosophy of farming had developed over years of study, of tilling the soil, of reading scholarly publications, of living the life, of looking back at past generations of his family who had worked the same land. His statement had blown me away, and I wasn't about to doubt the man for a second. But I couldn't, at this stage of what would turn out to be a wondrous schooling on the topic, quite comprehend it. Greg read me for a moment and said, "That's OK. To understand this properly will take time. So we're gonna introduce you to all the people you'll need to meet so that you can under-stand this – so that you can tell your story properly."

The Koethers' holistic grazing ranch lies in the unincorporated community of Giard, in northeast Iowa, about a 10-minute drive west of the Mississippi River from

McGregor. The ranch comprises 950 acres of owned pasture, 150 acres of rented pasture and 350 acres of timberland. It has 600 head of cattle, 400 head of sheep and 150 head of goats. To get there, you pass by a dilapidated old roadhouse that Greg said was full of bullet holes from long-dead drinkers and gamblers. Trucking right along, we passed a big grain bin operation called Northern Ag, an inviting greasy spoon called Maggie's Diner, and the occasional farmer out on his John Deere or International or Ford Powermaster tractor pulling an auger cart. I was learning the names of these farming implements as my education progressed.

The Koether Ranch had multiple houses, outbuildings and barns nestled among rolling green hills. We pulled under the shade of an old maple tree and got out. It was stifling in the sun, but in the shade of the maple, the air was cool and sweet. I stood and took stock of my surroundings, greeted by the chirping of cicadas, the barking of playful dogs and the sight of horses and mules and their stables not far off.

Greg and his family lived in a rambling, 1930s ranch-style house, which was all abustle in anticipation of the coming Field Day. So I was taken next-door to a hundred-and-something-year-old farmhouse. As I entered through the kitchen, I sensed a houseful of family memories: antiques, dried flowers and portraits of past Koethers. I offered to pitch my tent outside, but Greg insisted otherwise. This had been his parents' house, and because they had passed some time back, the place was unoccupied and ready to receive company.

> *It was such a charming home! – my new one; a fine great house, with pictures, and delicate decorations, and rich furniture, and no gloom anywhere, but all the wilderness of dainty colors lit up with flooding sunshine; and the spacious grounds around it, and the great garden – oh, greensward, and noble trees, and flowers, no end! And I was the same as a member of the family…*

—*The $30,000 Bequest*, 1874, Chapter 3

Kayla, the youngest of three Koether children, joined us for a tour of the house. She was in her first year of college at Grinnell, and seemed as passionate about sustainable farming as her father. She looked up to her dad admiringly as he showed me around the old homestead. There was the living room with two upright pianos that had been off-limits to the kids of past generations, "because we would have broken stuff," Greg explained. Upstairs was the "heirloom room," filled with family artifacts, books of poetry and volumes of the World Book Encyclopedia, which Kayla's grandparents had used to teach her about the wider world. The hallways and walls along the staircase were lined with portraits of ancestors who peered down as we passed. In a time when Americans are as transient as summertime clouds, I was struck by the notion that a family could live at the same spot for 160 years. Kayla was literally walking in the footsteps of her father.

The pictures on the walls harkened back to a time when

overalls were everyday garb, even on Sundays, and when nobody smiled for the camera. A portrait of Greg's great-grandfather, who had come to America from Ireland "with all of two nickels to rub together," hung in the kitchen.

"Peter headed out west to California aboard a clipper ship, passing at Panama, bound for the great Gold Rush," Greg said. "But realized early on only a few people were going to find gold." And so he tried something else, "driving oxen, sawing lumber, skidding lumber, selling lumber," in the end walking away with $8,000 in gold dust.

"Good old Peter traveled out of San Francisco on his horse, pretending to be down and out, flopping his flour sack of finely ground gold in clear sight of all at the odd roadhouse along the way, sleeping indoors and out, as if it were a sack of flour," Greg said. When Peter reached Iowa, land was going for $1.50 an acre. "Eight thousand dollars bought a lot of land back in 1853," Greg recounted. "Peter wanted to attain that dream of being the lord of all he could survey, with the goal to own everything out of the house, in all directions, as far as his eye could see."

My brother had just been appointed Secretary of Nevada Territory — an office of such majesty that it concentrated in itself the duties and dignities of Treasurer, Comptroller, Secretary of State, and Acting Governor in the Governor's absence. A salary of eighteen hundred dollars a year and the title of "Mr. Secretary," gave to the great position an air of wild and imposing grandeur. I was young and ignorant, and I envied my brother. I coveted his distinction and his financial splendor, but particularly and especially the long, strange journey he was going to make, and the curious new world he was going to explore. He was going to travel! I never had been away from home, and that word "travel" had a seductive charm for me. Pretty soon he would be hundreds and hundreds of miles away on the great plains and deserts, and among the mountains of the Far West, and would see buffaloes and Indians, and prairie dogs, and antelopes, and have all kinds of adventures, and may be get hanged or scalped, and have ever such a fine time, and write home and tell us all about it, and be a hero. And he would see the gold mines and the silver mines, and maybe go about of an afternoon when his work was done, and pick up two or three pailfuls of shining slugs, and nuggets of gold and silver on the hillside. And by and by he would become very rich, and return home by sea, and be able to talk as calmly about San Francisco and the ocean, and "the isthmus" as if it was nothing of any consequence to have seen those marvels face to face. What I suffered in contemplating his happiness, pen cannot describe. And so, when he offered me, in cold blood, the sublime position of private secretary under him, it appeared to me that the heavens and the earth passed away, and the firmament was rolled together as a scroll! I had nothing more to desire. My contentment was complete.

—*Roughing It*, 1872, Chapter 1

Older generations of Iowa farmers practiced a deeply embedded set of skills that were widely understood and shared. This was before World War II and the rise of chemical companies that in time would become seed companies. The Koethers and many other Iowa families had lived Peter's dream for a full century before the advent of the agricultural conglomerates. They shared a love of the land, lived in tightly knit communities and held to traditional values – family, church, hard work. That was before the world changed, with industrial farming and the promise of a "two-times yield."

On the morning of the field day, farmers of all varieties began to roll in at the Koether Ranch. I was introduced to conventional farmers, organic farmers, biodynamic farmers, fruit and vegetable farmers, dairy farmers, corn and soybean farmers, even the Amish.

Farmers from all over Iowa were gathering to see presentations on such topics as ways to make an operation chemical-free and how to build and nurture the soil. There were also demonstrations on sheepdog herding. What I was beginning to grasp is that there is a great divide between the thinking and practices of "conventional" farmers and "sustainable" farmers – and that the contest is very lopsided, with conventional farmers outnumbering sustainable farmers by about 98 to 2. I looked around and counted 50 to 60 folks who had come to hear the gospel of sustainability – and that was it. I wondered how they could possibly prevail.

Few people would probably argue against the merits and goals of sustainable and/or organic farming. Ideally, it results in safer food, untainted by chemicals, and better lives for the livestock and poultry that provide our meat. But it boils down to money, making a farming operation profitable. "You've got to do something besides building soil," farmer Craig Tritten noted during a question-and-answer session. "You've got to stay alive, too."

Greg Koether used a microphone as he led a tour of his land. In response to Tritten, he said he had taken his family ranch organic in 1982. "Hopefully, at the end of the day, at the end of the season," he said, "you put just as many pounds on those cattle, even though you've used them as a tool for a few days. The ground's better for it, and the cattle are as good or better than they would have been.

"Because you're thinking long-term and you're using a set of guidelines to make decisions," Greg went on, speaking of his "holistic" approach to farming. "And those guidelines are essential for the future of your farm, the community and the environment – especially in today's economic climate – in this ultimate pursuit of a goal that you've set out. That's what holistic resource management is all about."

I wondered: Were Greg Koether and the few like-minded holistic farmers the only ones questioning how most farms now operate? Were they the only ones looking at the big picture and the long-term impact of industrial farming on people and the environment? How long before the traditional family farm is completely snuffed out, along with everything that goes with it? Where had "conventional" farming techniques come from, and if they prevailed, what's next?

Those questions were still banging around in my head a few days later when I got a chance to visit the family farm of Norman Borlaug, an agronomist known as "the father of the Green Revolution" and winner of the Nobel Peace Prize in 1970.

The chain of fortuitous events that led to me visiting the Borlaug farm began when Mary Damm, a soil ecologist visiting from Indiana University, called Greg and said she would be doing some digging around Cresco, just up the road, and wondered if I'd like to see some virgin prairie. Greg asked if we could maybe do some digging on the Borlaug farm, also near Cresco. I thought he was joking, but Mary said, "Sure! Why not?" As it turned out, the man renting the Borlaug property for the past 20 years happened to be a friend. After another phone call, we not only had permission to dig, but I was invited to interview a neighbor of the Borlaug property who was the Nobel laureate's second cousin.

Greg and I sat at the Koether kitchen table as his wife, Kathy, served biscuits and gravy. "It's a subtle broadside, isn't it, I mean in the world of farming?" I asked Greg, wondering if the sustainability concept was as brilliant as I envisioned it at the time. Greg smiled, his hands clasped behind his neck, and replied, "Yes, Neal, it's a very subtle, overt broadside."

I had done a little research and knew who Norman

Borlaug was. (Uncannily, just 15 days after I filed my report on sustainable farming in Iowa to CNN, Borlaug died of lymphoma at age 95.) The Nobel Committee had said of Borlaug in its citation for the Peace Prize: "More than any other person of his age, he helped provide bread for a hungry world." Borlaug also won the Presidential Medal of Freedom and was the founder of the World Food Prize. According to Wikipedia, he was directly responsible for saving between 285 million and 1 billion lives from Mexico to India to Pakistan.

Partly because of Borlaug's work, the mantra in Iowa is that the state feeds the world. It has also become an unofficial motto of the multinational farming corporations.

I didn't wish to detract from the legacy of Borlaug, whose development of high-yield, disease-resistant grains led to the mass-production techniques used by the factory farms. But I wondered: How can the farming community as a whole strike a balance between tradition and innovation?

Thanks to the Natvig family, whose land neighbors the farm where Borlaug lived as a boy, the old Borlaug tract has been using sustainable farming techniques for the past 10 years. The Natvigs and Borlaugs, who trace their origins to Norway, have been neighbors as far back as they can remember, and they just happen to be related.

With the Natvigs' blessing, Mary Damm and I walked into the middle of the Borlaug land, now in pasture. Mary was in her element. To one side of the meadow was restored prairie; on the other side a group of black cows gazed placidly, knee-deep in native grass. I was eager to find out whether, after a decade of sustainable farming, the land would yield a trace of the chemical fertilizers and pesticides that had been used on it for 40 years, from 1960 to 2000. Mary's metal core sampler met with resistance as she pushed it into the soil, and she told me that was a bad sign. She wiped her forehead and tried again. Penetration of virgin prairie is much easier, she said, than the soil of an industrialized farm, where it's nearly impossible to obtain a core sample. She pushed and she pushed, and in the end we got our sample.

"The soil tells me that there have been some changes in the vegetation, I would say, for one," Mary said. "The soil here, the Borlaug Farm pasture soil, may not have the density of roots as the soil from the native prairie." It was interesting to note that, even with the reintroduction of native grasses and grazing cattle to mimic the buffalo that once roamed this land, the soil had not reverted to its native state. "Once chemicals have been introduced," Mary said, "it will never quite be the same."

When I asked Mary what that meant in layman's terms, she said, "Sustaining the soil means keeping the soil intact. And that's done with a perennial root system. So we have perennial roots in the native tall grass prairie, we have perennial roots in pasture grass, in a hay field, and once we have a perennial root system, that allows for the biological community and an entire food web to develop below ground."

Godfrey Natvig, 89, and his son Mike, 44, were hanging out on Godfrey's front porch, along with a plethora of tail-swishing cats. Godfrey had been born at the place – the sort of antiquated farmhouse that weekend artists try to conjure in watercolors. I joined them on the porch and we talked of conventional farming vs. sustainable farming.

Godfrey, a lifelong farmer and delightful fellow, had once been the Howard County soil and water commissioner. He and his son had used chemicals for several decades as they worked their land commercially. But they had decided to make not only their land but also the neighboring Borlaug property "sustainable." I wanted to know why.

"When I started farming there was no fertilizer or hybrid seed or weed spray," Godfrey said, breaking into an epic grin before chuckling. "So I guess we were organic farmers at that time – and didn't know it. The way the other people are doing it now, I think they're losing too much soil… It's washing away into the Mississippi. That's a big thing, I think."

I turned to Mike. He had observed Norman Borlaug's strategy firsthand. His famous cousin often came back to this very porch on visits and talked "about the work he was doing in these countries far away from Iowa." I asked Mike if we're starting to see a semblance of balance in farming techniques.

"I think we're still looking for it," Mike began, stroking his beard, taking his time. "I mean, I think you have to look back and follow some very basic principles of agriculture, and

I think a lot of those basic principles have been ignored for several years and I think we kind of need to look back … to achieve long-term sustainability."

I asked about surviving hard times, and turned to Godfrey. "What advice would you offer, looking back to the 1930s?" I asked. "How tough a go was it to survive in those times?"

He leaned forward and smiled. "Well, of course, as farmers we had milk, eggs, and meat," he said, speaking slowly and deliberately. "We were poor and we didn't know it. It's about the way it went. I didn't realize it till later that we were going through a depression. So it wasn't too bad for us – a lot of us. We didn't have a big debt or anything to pay off. We were doin' alright."

What about the future? I asked.

Godfrey shook his head from side to side before answering. "Well, it's hard to say, but recently they've been trying to farm thousands of acres – the big farmers. And they're kind of shutting out the smaller farmers that way. Whether they make any money or not, I don't know. It's questionable now, I think. Some are paying awful high rent at the present time with the cost of inputs they've got to pay. So I think there will be some changes in the future. I hope they'll be for the better."

The next morning I was helping with the chores, moving cattle between paddocks with Kayla and Greg, when we broke for breakfast at Maggie's Diner. We had these breakfasts nearly every morning at Maggie's, just down the road from the

Koether Ranch. Sometimes Kathy would join us, sometime the Koethers' youngest son, Klint, and Klint's girlfriend, Kelli. It was the most wonderful of rituals. We'd drink bottomless cups of coffee and talk about life in general: about how Greg hadn't been to church in a long while because he preferred to worship Emily Dickinson-style, with the bobolinks, the blackbirds that flit about the ranch; about how Kathy knew the talents and aspirations of everyone in several Iowa counties because she had taught them as kids and now was a school principal; about how Klint and Kelli didn't think they could stay too long away from this land even though they might have opportunities further afield than McGregor; about how Kayla had designed her own major at Grinnell and was looking forward to a program of study in Mongolia.

Yes, this was a family of American farmers. But they certainly didn't represent a stereotype. Like all of us, they had hopes, faults, fears and a certain pride – a pride that has less to do with symbols, like the American flag, and more to do with a genuine interest in and concern for society at large. They were comfortable, yet inquisitive, and it seemed that their thirst for knowledge was an ongoing concern.

The family was curious about my experience on the Borlaug farm and I was eager to share, as well as to learn their views on the differences between the hard times of the 1930s and those today. How will a sustained economic slump play out? I asked. The responses of father and daughter surprised me.

"I think it's ironic that here in Iowa we do grow so many crops, but that if tomorrow we weren't able to buy food, nobody would be able to eat anything that's in the fields," Kayla said. "We'd essentially starve. We're no better off than a desert that can't grow anything.

"So it's kind of interesting that … we like to call ourselves the breadbasket of the world and say we feed the world, but we couldn't feed ourselves if it really came right down to it. And that's not because we don't have intelligent people or amazing resources. It's because of what we're growing and how we grow it – it's not edible."

Greg chimed in, as if on cue: "An economist, Ken Meter, did a study for the five-county area here in northeast Iowa. He calculated the value of the commercially grown crops – in other words, the corn, soybeans, dairy and beef – that were leaving the five-county area. He then calculated the amount of food that was being purchased by the people living in the five-county area. Huge discrepancy.

"The value of the corn and soybeans that was being sold was much less than the value of the food being purchased in, if you don't figure in government subsidies," Greg said. "We're not even feeding ourselves in this five-county area and we should be eating the best, and, basically, what it boils down to is local foods would serve this area much better than the food that's being trucked in from miles and miles away.

"It was a huge shock to me," Greg said. "When you look

at all these productive fields and things, they're not producing the value of the food that the people that are living here are eating – and we've been losing population for years and years. I thought certainly that our population would not be eating anywhere near that amount that the prices indicate. If we could just feed ourselves with local food, that would be a huge improvement. Just that alone."

I learned more during the ride to a barn dance held that Friday night on the other side of McGregor. We all hopped into the family minivan, and before we got out of the driveway the drinks began to flow. It struck me as oddly hilarious that we had a makeshift minibar operating in the back of a minivan. Jeff Mueller, a family friend and local farmhand, was busily wrangling the ice and somebody else was pouring the Black Velvets. Every time we hit a bump, the ice clinked wildly and we laughed and raised our oversized plastic cups. Jeff sported a fine cavalry hat, complete with a Jesus pin and a yellow cord around the bottom of the crown. Kathy was dressed to the nines in a shiny blue getup that glinted in the evening light. It felt great to be on the move, and it felt liberating to be breaking the law, along with everyone else, save for the driver. We held our plastic cups in the air, smiled broadly and toasted the night.

It's hard to put into words how it felt to be headed to a dance with a family of farmers, everybody all dressed up. I cradled on my lap a shotgun that I had received as a gift from the Koethers, worried that I'd soon be back on the river by myself and might need protection. Earlier that evening, someone had asked if I was carrying a gun during my trip. When I said no, Greg went downstairs and came back toting a Snake Charmer, a .410 shotgun with a short barrel, easy to stow in a canoe. He took the shotgun out onto the porch and fired once into the air, then pulled back a lever to eject the spent shell, and fired again. "That will do you," he said. "That will keep you safe."

I'll never be a member of the National Rifle Association or much of a dancer. But that Friday night was intoxicating, and it had little to do with the alcoholic lubrication. I came to McGregor for a story, and I found friends. I was no longer a stranger here; I felt like family. These people had accepted me. That night I felt like I never wanted to leave – that I could spend the rest of my life on the Koether Ranch and its environs and that it would be a fine existence indeed.

I told my hosts as we drove to the dance that I felt as if I'd stepped into a John Steinbeck novel, *The Grapes of Wrath*, that the Koethers were like the Joad family in an earlier period of hard times and that Americans like me were wondering how things would all turn out this time around. I slipped back into journalist mode and asked if the multinational farming corporations of today were like the banks of the Joads' time and if small farmers like the Koethers would point a finger of blame.

"No one can hold it accountable," Greg said, referring to

the agricultural-industrial complex. "The family farm equals wage labor. We call it wage labor because nobody owns their own business anymore. You don't have access to certain things in the marketplace that you want.

"If you follow the rules of commercial farming, and go along with the right type of hybrid seed and resistance seed, the seed you buy now, you have to buy the chemicals to go along with. You're not a true independent businessman because you don't have choice in the marketplace anymore – from either side. Purchasing or selling."

At the dance, we met up with Klint and Kelli and a few of their friends and our party got bigger. The barn was decked out in lights and folks were already whirling about on the dance floor, its planks strewn with sawdust.

I was exceedingly delighted with the waltz, and also with the polka. These differ in name, but there the difference ceases – the dances are precisely the same. You have only to spin around with frightful velocity and steer clear of the furniture. This has a charming and bewildering effect. You catch glimpses of a confused and whirling multitude of people, and above them a row of distracted fiddlers extending entirely around the room. The waltz and the polka are very exhilarating – to use a mild term – amazingly exhilarating.

—From a letter to the *Territorial Enterprise, Dec. 12, 1862*

Greg and Kathy, Kayla and Jeff and Klint and Kelli made several forays onto the floor and danced to the music of a local band called Southern Comfort. At one point, between drinks,

I loosened up and confided to Greg that my brother, who died when I was a kid, had dated the daughter of one of the Eagles, and that I missed him terribly. I was in a bit of a daze amid the noise of laughter, shuffling feet and clinking glasses and I hardly noticed that Southern Comfort was launching into another song. Greg leaned toward me and said, "This is the Eagles." The band had transitioned from "Seven Bridges Road" to "Take It Easy," an Eagles classic. I was about to feel sorry for myself when I looked up and was struck by the sheer exuberance of the occasion – the band, the music, the company. Everybody was dancing and having a good time. Against my better judgment, I got up from the table and thrust myself into the fray.

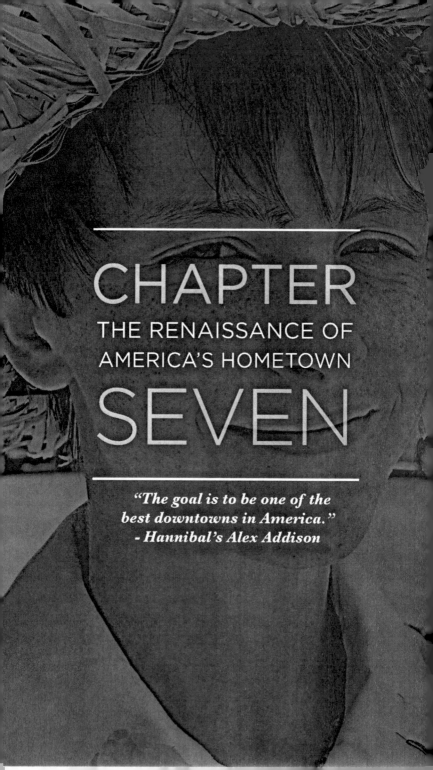

CHAPTER

THE RENAISSANCE OF
AMERICA'S HOMETOWN

SEVEN

"The goal is to be one of the
best downtowns in America."
- Hannibal's Alex Addison

I NOTICED THE KID at the Casey's convenience store when the lady behind the counter said she didn't know if the town had a restaurant. It was late, about 10 p.m., in La Grange, Mo. I'd come off the river for the night and spotted a yellow neon sign that I hoped marked the location of a hotel or restaurant, because I hadn't had a proper meal or a good night's rest for a long time. But the sign was for a Casey's, so I bought a ready-made pizza.

Well, when Tom and me got to the edge of the hill-top we looked away down into the village and could see three or four lights twinkling, where there was sick folks, maybe; and the stars over us was sparkling ever so fine; and down by the village was the river, a whole mile broad, and awful still and grand.

—*Adventures of Huckleberry Finn*, 1885, Chapter 2

The boy walked behind me in the store and tried to make conversation, but the lady cut him off. I figured he might know something about the lay of the land, like where I might find a place to eat and sleep. So I followed him when he left the store. One thing I'd learned on this trip: always listen to the locals, especially advice on navigating the river. The boy asked me my name and I told him "Neal." He seemed to be about the same age as Huckleberry Finn, which would make him about 13. But his face and eyes made him look older and wiser than his years. He introduced himself as "Thomas."

"We've both got accents," Thomas said with a grin. "I'm from New Jersey. Where are you from?" I should have said L.A., but I told him I was from the river. He wanted to see my canoe and told me to stay off La Grange Island, a large island just opposite the town where I had earlier tried to land. "That place is haunted – tons of ghosts running around there at night," Thomas said. Looking at the wooded island in the dark did indeed give me the creeps, and the night calls of birds wafting across the narrow channel added to the island's eeriness.

Thomas asked again about the canoe, which he was eager to check out. On the walk back to the river, I asked him what he thought about Hannibal, my next planned stop, just a day's paddle downriver. He said he liked Hannibal and said his own town, La Grange, was "sleepy."

When he saw the canoe, Thomas pronounced it a "good one" and asked if it had a name. "No," I said. "I tried really hard to come up with a good one early on but for the life of me, just couldn't." I thought for a moment, and asked the obvious question: "What do you think? What does she look like to you?" Thomas took a step back and thought for a moment. He scratched his head and then his whiskerless chin, likean old man trying to decide whether to buy a tractor.

After thinking a good, long while, he said: "The Andrea. How about the Andrea?" Not in a million years would I have thought to call my Old Town canoe the Andrea. But now that Thomas said it, it sounded right. "The Andrea it is," I said in a booming voice, sounding out the name loud and clear to make sure it sounded right.

"Alright," Thomas said. "But you can't go and change the name now. That's bad luck. We learned that in Boy Scouts."

As we talked, the boy's half of the conversation was laden with allusions to death, ghosts and luck, good and bad. He seemed to know a great deal about the river and Hannibal, the boyhood home of Mark Twain and a town that surely had a few ghosts of its own.

The boy's jet-black hair set off his face, which appeared spectral in the moonlight. He walked away briefly, disappearing in the darkness. When he came back, he leaned forward, as if to confide a great secret. "There was a barge that caught fire right over there – and everyone died," the boy said, pointing a finger to a spot just down the river. "Everyone died."

I looked to the spot, as if searching for the barge's smoldering hulk, and he pointed again, "Right over there."

I set down my lantern at the prow of the canoe, stowed my bag and put the pizza box on one of the canoe's cane seats. The encounter with the boy was making me uneasy. I should have shaken hands with Thomas, offered him a slice of pizza or snapped his picture, as I had with nearly everyone else I met along the river. But I didn't – and I didn't quite know why. Was I afraid that he might not be real, that he might be one of the many specters said to haunt the river?

Thomas spoke as if he came from a different time. He told the story of the barge fire as if it had just happened. "These barges are dangerous," he said. "This one ended up killing everyone on board. They're going to make a plaque."

The river's earliest commerce was in great barges – keelboats, broad horns. They floated and sailed from the upper rivers to New Orleans, changed cargoes there, and were tediously warped and poled back by hand. A voyage down and back sometimes occupied nine months. In time this commerce increased until it gave employment to hordes of rough and hardy men; rude, uneducated, brave, suffering terrific hardships with sailor-like stoicism; heavy drinkers, coarse frolickers in moral sties like the Natchez-under-the-hill of that day, heavy fighters, reckless fellows, every one, elephantinely jolly, foul-witted, profane; prodigal of their money, bankrupt at the end of the trip, fond of barbaric finery, prodigious braggarts; yet, in the main, honest, trustworthy, faithful to promises and duty, and often picturesquely magnanimous.

—*Life on the Mississippi*, 1883, Chapter 3

Thomas was full of advice about the hazards on the Mississippi. He told me about barges moored in the river off Quincy, Ill. – about halfway between La Grange and Hannibal – and about other dangers that only a local would know about. He wished me well and told me where to camp on Hogback Island, a mile or two downriver. "Over on the lee side where there is a spot of sand," he said. I asked if Deadman's Island, next to Hogback, was haunted like La Grange. "Oh, yeah, wickedly haunted," he said. "There was a yacht and a sailboat and they crashed and all but one died. Also, there's this thick fog that always hangs around the place, so you don't see it until it's too late."

"And Hogback Island *isn't* haunted?" I asked, wanting to make sure that no ghosts would be lounging about where I had decided to camp for the night. "No. That one's not

haunted," Thomas said. "You can camp there alright."
So Hogback it would be.

I felt comfortable with the choice because the
lockmaster at Keokuk Lock and Dam No. 19, upriver at
Keokuk, Iowa, had also told me that Hogback would be
a good place to spend a night. With the lantern fixed to
the bow, my canoe drifted into the night, away from
the hamlet of La Grange. The canoe moved silently in the
still water, but the cacophony of the crickets and the
birds reminded me of the Pirates of the Caribbean ride at
Disneyland. It was delightfully creepy. When I looked back to
wave to Thomas, he was gone.

*I was away below the ferry now. I rose up, and there was Jackson's
Island, about two mile and a half down stream, heavy timbered
and standing up out of the middle of the river, big and dark and
solid, like a steamboat without any lights. There warn't any signs
of the bar at the head — it was all under water now.*

*It didn't take me long to get there. I shot past the head at a ripping
rate, the current was so swift, and then I got into the dead water and
landed on the side towards the Illinois shore. I run the canoe into
a deep dent in the bank that I knowed about; I had to part the
willow branches to get in; and when I made fast nobody could
a seen the canoe from the outside.*

*I went up and set down on a log at the head of the island, and
looked out on the big river and the black driftwood and away over*

to the town, three mile away, where there was three or four lights twinkling. A monstrous big lumber-raft was about a mile up stream, coming along down, with a lantern in the middle of it. I watched it come creeping down, and when it was most abreast of where I stood I heard a man say, "Stern oars, there! heave her head to stabboard!" I heard that just as plain as if the man was by my side.

There was a little gray in the sky now; so I stepped into the woods, and laid down for a nap before breakfast.

—*Adventures of Huckleberry Finn*, 1885, Chapter 7

When you camp on the islands in the Mississippi River, you come to understand that a lot of these places have a rich history. The first island that I camped on was Battle Island, just upriver from Victory, Wis. I was told after I slept there that at least 150 Sauk and Fox Indians were massacred on and near the island in 1832 by U.S. Army regulars and militia during the Black Hawk War. I spent a peaceful night on Battle Island. But other island camping spots were not so tranquil, like the one a couple nights back that had trees so ancient and ominous that I didn't want to land anywhere near the place. I did so only out of necessity. The wind in the trees that night sounded like some forest critter was running up and down on my tent.

When morning broke on Hogback Island, the sky was blindingly bright, yet chockablock with scudding, tumbling clouds that reminded me of Alan Paton's "fairest, green rolling valleys" of Natal Province in South Africa. "These hills are grass-covered and rolling, and they are lovely beyond any singing of it," Paton wrote in his novel *Cry, The Beloved Country.*

That day, I was supposed to meet with members of the Hannibal Chamber of Commerce at a designated time and place, but I had been distracted by the loveliness of the world around me and was off to a late start. I couldn't get a cellphone signal at my campsite to advise my hosts that I might be delayed, so I had to paddle hard to make up for lost time. I paid special attention to the barges and waved at the towboat captains. Some of them ducked out of their wheelhouses to wave back. Mark Twain was on my mind as I paddled beneath the two bridges just upriver from Hannibal, and I scanned the eastern shore looking for Jackson's Island, made famous by Twain's *Adventures of Huckleberry Finn.* I couldn't find it on my map.

I was giddy as I paddled up to the town, stirred by respect for the steamboat pilot-turned-author whose characters were drawn from folks who walked Hannibal's streets 170 years ago. You can't paddle the Mississippi without paying homage, I had told myself, so when I strode along Hannibal's Main Street, just up from the river landing, I felt like I was ingesting a huge dose of Americana. A tonic, Aunt Polly might have said. I took big breaths, trying to take it all in.

I found no one from the Chamber of Commerce waiting for me, so I trudged along Main, my Muck Boots, scraggly beard and sunburned nose marking me as someone who had just come off the river. I hadn't taken a shower since Iowa, and I looked and felt like a down-and-outer. Then on the sidewalk I ran into Frank Salter, the chamber representative, and I felt a bit more respectable. We shook hands and talked a bit as we walked, river water still sloshing around in my boots. Soon I was ushered into the Mark Twain Boyhood Home & Museum.

I was surprised by the mini-reception that awaited me. Museum staff and townsfolk lined up to shake my hand, and then I was introduced with ceremony befitting a visiting dignitary to the ambassadors of the town, Thomas Sawyer and Rebecca Thatcher.

This Tom was different from the one I'd met the previous night at La Grange. He said he wasn't a Boy Scout and that he liked to play golf in his free time. But Alex Addison, this 13-year-old, freckle-faced ambassador of Hannibal, anointed by the Chamber of Commerce, was all business. For his role as Tom Sawyer, he went barefoot and wore a frayed straw hat and knee-length britches. As we were introduced, he leaned toward me confidentially and said: "If you need me to miss school, again, say for an interview or such, that can most certainly be arranged."

Paige Cummins, the beaming, bonneted Becky, murmured, "Oh, Tom!" and blushed convincingly. Her gloved hands grasped her calico skirts as she flirted, curtsied and scolded

Tom for playing hooky. Waylon Jennings was right: "Ladies love outlaws."

I had a hunch that following "Tom Sawyer" around Hannibal would make for a pretty good story about the place that calls itself "America's Hometown." So, the next day I met up with Alex, who took me on a tour with the polish of a professional politician. Away from the museum, he dropped his "Tom Sawyer" schtick and became Alex. We talked about real life in Hannibal during this time of economic woe, and he offered a perspective seen through the optimistic eyes of youth. He said that his parents owned a handful of buildings and businesses along Main Street, which gave him some insight into how the economy works. When asked what he thought about the economic downturn, from his family's perspective, Alex said: "I see it not as a challenge but as a goal – and the goal is to be one of the best downtowns in America ... which I think we can really reach. I mean, how many downtowns have as much history and nice people and businesses? It's starting to click. It's going to be really good."

Steve Ayers, who has been a downtown merchant for 25 years, offered a slightly different view. "It's just one step forward and two back," said Ayers, who owns Java Jive, a coffee shop and pottery that calls itself "the first coffee shop west of the Mississippi." "And then one step forward and a foot back and now we're about even. Little by little – it's like small business anywhere else. People have a dream and put their life savings and their kids' college funds into it."

On my second day in Hannibal, Steve Ayers and I had picked up the tour of the town where Alex Addison, a.k.a. Tom Sawyer, had left off. As we walked down Main Street with my video camera rolling, he showed me what businesses had succeeded and recounted the histories of those that had failed. When we passed Java Jive, I noticed that his own shop was full of both tourists and locals.

Later, I met with a group of blue-collar guys chewing the fat at a barbershop on the other side of town, away from the downtown tourist sites. I thought it would be a good location for a story I planned to call "Straight talk with a straight shave." But I was a bit taken aback when one of the men said: "Tell CNN that we don't want everybody over there in the downtown district shingling up the name of Mark Twain."

Hannibal has had a hard time of it ever since I can recollect, and I was "raised" there. First, it had me for a citizen, but I was too young then to really hurt the place.

—*Letter to the Alta California*, May 26, 1867

"Sure thing," I told the man, maybe too glibly. But I understood what he meant. There are two sides to Hannibal, like other river towns I had passed through. This side, where most people worked for wages, comprised the majority of the population. They had trouble identifying with tourism, historic preservation and Mark Twain's literary legacy because they felt there wasn't much in it for them. Many had worked for industries in decline or in factories already idle and boarded up.

On the other side were the "progressives," who pushed the cause of historic preservation like evangelists for a new religion. These folks, by and large, were transplants from other walks of life or other places who liked to call Hannibal a "village." They were doing their best to beautify and preserve a vision of old Hannibal, restoring a charm that had faded in previous decades. They were busy renovating the baseball stadium and an old theater, reconstructing a wonderfully varied string of mom-and-pop shops along Main Street, raising money to preserve and restore – count 'em – eight Mark Twain museum properties, all the while extending the "historic district" into the rows of once-grand houses where lumber barons had lived just up from the main drag.

One of those old houses, now beautifully restored to its 1870s splendor, is the Dubach Inn on Fifth Street, where I lodged the first three nights of my stay in Hannibal. The inn's proprietors, Steve and Kristine Russell, like many in the neighborhood, were transplants. They came from Washington state, where Steve had lost his job in a factory before starting his own landscaping company. He sold that business to help finance the move to Hannibal. "When we looked at the value of our house out west and what we could buy in Hannibal, and the fact we just might have a source of income by opening a bed and breakfast, coupled with a historic dream house to grow old in, it just made sense," Kristine said. "So we went ahead and made the move and bought the house, sight unseen."

But the economy didn't cooperate. They didn't get as much as they had hoped from their house in Washington. And even with a fairly steady flow of travelers coming to the front door of the Dubach, Steve had to find part-time work just out of town. Nevertheless, the Russells were making their dream work, and they were content. "It could have been a whole lot worse," they said. The Russells were wonderfully optimistic about life in general and were deeply into "preservation." When I suggested that this seemed to be the engine of the town's economy, they took me next-door to meet Bob Yapp, a TV and radio personality who dispenses advice on restoring old buildings.

After traveling the country as an expert on historic preservation, with shows on affiliates of National Public Radio and the Public Broadcasting Service, Yapp decided to settle for good in Hannibal. He said he had been drawn to the town because of "a love for Hannibal's architecture." He shook my hand with a broad smile, the sort you'd expect from a guy with a TV show. I'd heard about his work with Hannibal's at-risk youth and his hands-on high school class that teaches the manual skills needed in historic preservation. And I wanted to cover it.

We sat on the steps of his front porch, which was being

recreated by his manual arts students to look exactly like it did in a 19th-century oil painting of the house. "Across the nation, small communities are reinventing themselves," Yapp said. "They're having a renaissance in the sense that factories move out – things change. And the towns that don't take the time to reinvent themselves are the towns that don't survive."

The next day, at Yapp's house, I watched as a handful of Hannibal High kids gathered around a power saw as he showed them how to use it. "I actually want to do exactly what Bob is doing," one girl said. "When you're here you actually get to do stuff and work on stuff that you actually want to do." Another student, Christian, got misty-eyed when I asked why he was so passionate about his work in the class. "I want to be like my dad," he said. "He was a carpenter. I want to make him proud."

The kids, most of whom said they wanted to work in historic preservation when they graduated, were building a fence at Yapp's house the day I interviewed them. The house, the second-largest in Hannibal, had once been a hangout for drug dealers. Yapp and his students were returning it to its past glory.

I had saved for last my meeting with Dr. Cindy Lovell, executive director of the Mark Twain Boyhood Home & Museum, partly because she was so busy and partly because I saw my meeting with her as the most important of my Hannibal visit. By the time it took place, the local newspaper, the *Hannibal Courier-Post,* apparently agreed. The paper had picked up on my journey down the river and its reporters took notes and snapped photos as I met with Dr. Lovell in her museum office.

I hadn't yet realized it, but in Hannibal, *my* story was becoming theirs. The next day, I found myself smiling out of the paper's front page, with the headline: "CNN reporter: Hannibal is most certainly America's Hometown."

Dr. Lovell spoke during our meeting of the "lessons to be learned in the preservation of our past," and she invited me to continue the conversation about preserving Sam Clemens' legacy over dinner at LulaBelle's, once a riverfront bordello and now one of Hannibal's best restaurants. As our dinner conversation shifted from one topic to another, we discovered a common bond: each of us had lost a brother. Feeling a tinge sentimental, I described my nighttime encounter in La Grange with Thomas and his warnings about ghosts.

Then I heard myself making a preposterous proposal: "What would you say if I asked if you'd like to go up Cardiff Hill tonight, say around about the witching hour, up at the cemetery, to take a look around." To which Cindy – we were now on a first-name basis – leaned across the table, pushed aside the candle between us and said: "I'd say that would be the most exciting thing I've done in a very long time."

It was a graveyard of the old-fashioned Western kind. It was on a hill, about a mile and a half from the village. It had a crazy board fence around it, which leaned inward in places, and outward the rest of the time, but stood upright nowhere. Grass and weeds grew rank over the whole cemetery. All the old graves were sunken in, there was not a tombstone on the place; round-topped, worm-eaten boards staggered over the graves, leaning for support and finding none. "Sacred to the memory of" So-and-So had been painted on them once, but it could no longer have been read, on the most of them, now, even if there had been light.

—*The Adventures of Tom Sawyer*, 1876, Chapter 9

Equipped with flashlights, we made our way to the small summit at the northern end of Hannibal that served as a playground, a place of refuge and a site of boyhood intrigue for Tom Sawyer and Huckleberry Finn. There might have been a "Keep Out" sign at the Old Baptist Cemetery on the eastern side of Cardiff Hill, but in the dark we didn't see it as we walked amid the graves of town luminaries and at least one slave – Agness Flautleroy, who died in 1855. She had been owned by Sophia Hawkins, mother of Laura Hawkins, who was Mark Twain's model for Becky Thatcher.

To walk in the footsteps of young Sam Clemens, to peer into the darkness and see what he saw, to imagine what childhood fears Sam and Tom Blankenship, the real Huckleberry Finn, had to overcome as they set out on their nocturnal excursions to this place of the dead was a thrill I'll not soon forget.

As Cindy and I crouched among the gravestones swapping stories, I recounted a conversation I had with my friends in Iowa about how utterly cool it would be to pitch my tent outside one of the museum properties. My friends scoffed at this fanciful idea, one of them screeching: "Neal, that will NEVER happen!" Cindy smiled, and looked as if she were turning an idea over in her head. "Well, maybe not a tent, but what about sleeping in the boyhood home?" she asked. "In Sam Clemens' own room?" I think she was as surprised to hear herself offer the invitation as I was to hear it. I didn't give her a second to reconsider: "I'd say that would be positively insane!"

We worked out the details, and it was decided that I'd spend an extra night in Hannibal – my last – in the upper, back bedroom of the Mark Twain Boyhood Home, Sam Clemens' room. We would make a news story of it and bill the event as "Modern-day Huck to sleep in Mark Twain's Boyhood Home tonight!" Cindy's logic is guided by the question: "What would Mark Twain want me to do?" I'm sure she convinced herself that offering lodging to a wayfaring river rat was in keeping with the spirit of Hannibal's most famous son. But she also had one eye keenly fixed on the constant challenge of raising awareness – and money – for the museum properties.

Many a small thing has been made large by the right kind of advertising.

—*A Connecticut Yankee in King Arthur's Court,* 1889, Chapter 22

My sleepover would kick off a drive to raise donations to the museum's endowment fund. The aim was to reach Mark Twain fans near and afar and persuade them to donate $10 each to become virtual signers of "Tom Sawyer's Fence" outside Twain's boyhood home. Cindy looked at the museum records and found that I would be the first person in 50 years to spend a night in Sam Clemens' bedroom, and only the second in the nearly 100 years that the house had been preserved as a museum.

"Sam Clemens began his career as something of a citizen journalist, contributing pieces when and where he could," the museum's news release said. "Neal's adventure, his story within a story, resonated with us. Like Twain, he is a reporter. Like Huck, he is an adventurer. He symbolizes the spirit we are trying to preserve." I was to be the first Twain fan to donate $10 and sign my name to the whitewashed fence.

The event was covered by local affiliates of NBC and ABC, Ed Husar of the *Quincy Herald-Whig* and Danny Henley of the *Courier-Post*. At the appointed hour, a small crowd of townspeople and curious tourists gathered in the rain to watch me enter the boyhood home. It's possible that I'd been this excited before in my life, but I must have been a child then and don't remember it.

Amid hugs and handshakes in the rain, I bade goodnight to my new friends in Hannibal who had turned up for the event, to Richard Garey, a local actor who impersonates

Mark Twain, and to the soaking-wet passers-by who were curious enough to stick around. I went inside to find that a local inn had delivered an elegant five-course meal. As I dined by candlelight in the Clemens' kitchen, the food seemed exponentially delicious because of the setting. I finished the meal with the last few sips from a fifth of Southern Comfort that I had in my bag, and said to myself over and over: "I cannot believe this is happening." If the Lincoln Bedroom was available to wealthy donors for $10,000 a night during Bill Clinton's presidency, I wondered what Cindy could charge for this. "You cannot attach a price to it," I said, sounding like a credit card commercial as I looked into my laptop's iSight lens recording a video report on my sleepover, "for this is a moment that is quite simply priceless."

I laid out my bedding on the bedroom floor, but was too excited to sleep. So I read for about an hour from The Adventures of Tom Sawyer. Sam Clemens lived in this house from age 4 to 17. At the time, life on the western frontier could be brutish and short. Death was a common occurrence – from disease, violence, drowning. Mark Twain later wrote that as a boy in Hannibal he received news of every death as a warning from Providence. In this very room, he wrestled with his conscience at night and vowed to mend his ways – at least until morning.

With the going down of the sun my faith failed and the clammy fears gathered about my heart. It was then that I repented. Those were awful nights, nights of despair, nights charged with the bitterness of death. After each tragedy I recognized the warning and repented; repented and begged; begged like a coward, begged like a dog; and not in the interest of those poor people who had been extinguished for my sake, but only in my own interest. It seems selfish, when I look back on it now.

My repentances were very real, very earnest; and after each tragedy they happened every night for a long time. But as a rule they could not stand the daylight. They faded out and shredded away and disappeared in the glad splendor of the sun. They were the creatures of fear and darkness, and they could not live out of their own place. The day gave me cheer and peace, and at night I repented again. In all my boyhood life I am not sure that I ever tried to lead a better life in the daytime – or wanted to. In my age I should never think of wishing to do such a thing. But in my age, as in my youth, night brings me many a deep remorse. I realize that from the cradle up I have been like the rest of the race – never quite sane in the night.

—*Mark Twain's Autobiography*, 1924, Chapter 5

And then it was morning. It was the first day of autumn and the air was sweet and peaceful. I looked up from where I lay to the back bedroom window, the one that young Sam used to escape from the house for nighttime rambles. Then I looked to my left and saw a window that I had failed to notice in the dark the previous night. This side window, I suddenly re-alized, provided the view that shaped his imagination. There, directly ahead was Main Street, and just beyond was the Mississippi River.

CHAPTER
MOVING
POSITIVE
EIGHT

Building homes,
Jeff-Vander-Lou, St. Louis

THE MISSISSIPPI RIVER reveals herself in stages. First, it's the beauty. On any given day, in weather fair or foul, the river offers vistas as breathtaking as any to be found in North America. As you get to know the river better, you begin to discover her many moods and learn to accept that there will be many twists and turns along the Mississippi's journey to the sea.

The river's meandering, sometimes unpredictable course was a reflection of my own personal journey and ever-changing moods. I put on a brave face for my friends in Hannibal as I waved goodbye at the town's marina and set out again on the river.

> *The day after, when we rose up toward the sky and sailed off eastward, we looked back and watched that place till it warn't nothing but just a speck… and I tell you it was like saying good-bye to a friend that you ain't ever going to see any more.*

—*Tom Sawyer Abroad, 1894,* Chapter 9

I waited for that great emptiness to hit me, the realization that yet again I was completely on my own. But that feeling didn't come. Instead, I felt – and it may seem fanciful – that from this spot forward I was no longer alone. I was now traveling, if only in my mind's eye, with Sam and Jim and Huck. The four of us were in the canoe and we were paddling for all we were worth, smiling at the wonder of it all.

The stories that I would tell from now on would take on multiple layers. They would be imbued with the aspirations and viewpoints of Jim and of Huck and their creator, Mark Twain. Together, we'd be talking about some of America's undercurrents: race relations, the plight of runaway and abused children, illiteracy – and we'd be visiting a prison.

But for now St. Louis beckoned. I had been in touch with Courtney Simms, director of resources for the largest Habitat for Humanity affiliate in the nation, Habitat for Humanity St. Louis. The story of the group's work in the historic Jeff-Vander-Lou neighborhood had fascinated me from the moment I learned of it. A community was being reborn in a wasteland of vacant lots, boarded-up buildings and faded dreams. Jeff-Vander-Lou, just northwest of downtown, takes its name from the three avenues that African-Americans used to get to work downtown – Jefferson, Vandeventer and St. Louis. In the time of racial segregation following the abolition of slavery, Jeff-Vander-Lou was designated as St. Louis's "Negro District" and was one of the few places where blacks were allowed to own residential and commercial real estate.

The neighborhood had once flourished, but as factories closed and jobs disappeared its people began to move away. For those who were left, Jeff-Vander-Lou was a place of poverty, drug-dealing and violent crime.

London was fifteen hundred years old, and was a great town – for that day. It had a hundred thousand inhabitants – some think double as many. The streets were very narrow, and crooked, and dirty, especially in the part where Tom Canty lived...

The house which Tom's father lived in was up a foul little pocket called Offal Court, out of Pudding Lane. It was small, decayed, and rickety, but it was packed full of wretchedly poor families. Canty's tribe occupied a room on the third floor. The mother and father had a sort of bedstead in the corner; but Tom, his grandmother, and his two sisters, Bet and Nan, were not restricted – they had all the floor to themselves, and might sleep where they chose. There were the remains of a blanket or two, and some bundles of ancient and dirty straw, but these could not rightly be called beds, for they were not organized; they were kicked into a general pile mornings, and selections made from the mass at night, for service…

—*The Prince and the Pauper,* 1882, Chapter 2

Alfton Denise Jackson is a black single mother with hopes of a better life – mostly for the sake of her two sons, Alexander, 12, and Ledra, 7. Their apartment building, where we met, bordered on what she called a slum. "St. Louis is trying to build up around here but we're right next to some of the projects," she said. "It's somewhat scary. But although we have learned to cope with it, it's not a place I would want to raise my kids because it's kind of dangerous." Asked if he was afraid of living in this part of the city, Alexander replied, "Yes. There was a shooting. There are gunshots nearby that ring out in the night."

Like many working-class Americans, Ms. Jackson has been affected by the economic slump. "A couple of years ago I had lost my job and I was out of work for about six months and I really was having a hard time – even providing things for my boys," she said. "But we made it through because I just kept myself motivated. And now we're headed, we're moving positive."

The next day I met with Courtney Simms, who was heading up the Habitat St. Louis project in Jeff-Vander-Lou. It was a Saturday and, for the moment, the sky was bright and sunny, and all around us a community was busy putting itself back together. She spoke of the history of Jeff-Vander-Lou: "It wasn't just the first African-American homes of the city, but the first African-American-owned businesses, down in the corridor, a couple of blocks over. So to be able to come into this neighborhood and build homes is quite significant."

Ms. Simms directed me to an all-terrain vehicle and offered to take me on a tour. We tooled around Jeff-Vander-Lou, driving up one street and down another, watching hundreds of volunteers reclaim their neighborhood's history and lost pride. We stopped occasionally so I could speak to volunteers and to residents of some of the old apartment blocks. "Habitat and community – well, I think they're synonymous," one volunteer said. Another, Mark Roberts Sr., a corporate vice president, said he was a 14-year veteran with Habitat for Humanity. Asked what advice he'd give to others who wanted to get involved, he said, "I guess I'd encourage everyone to get out and do something in the community, maybe participation in Habitat, maybe working at the local food bank, maybe just helping out a neighbor who's struggling – particularly in today's environment."

Another volunteer, Bob, described the looks on the faces of families who step into a new home for the first time in their lives, a home that they now own. "There's always been tears – and that's just me," Bob said. "I mean the homebuyer, oftentimes, they're in tears, too. And it makes it all worthwhile.

"No matter how many days you're out there in the heat,"

Bob continued, "no matter how many days you're out there trudging through mud, no matter how many days you hit your thumb with a hammer, when it comes to that dedication day, you see the little kids of the homeowner and they say, 'Thanks for helping my mom build her house.' And you can't help but come back the following year."

During our tour, I was delighted to come across Alfton Jackson, wearing a hard hat and swinging away with a hammer. I took out my camera and captured the moment. She was all smiles, and her face radiated joy and hope. I asked her what she thought about the prospect of owning a home. She looked up to the heavens and said: "Thank you, Jesus!"

Ms. Jackson was working that day with her Habitat mentor, Wendy McPherson, who had gone through the process of building and buying her first home via Habitat for Humanity in 2006 and now lived just down the street. Ms. McPherson explained her role.

"Basically, just sharing advice and comfort," she said. "You know, just making sure Alfton's all right. It's a first-time experience for a lot of us, being, becoming homeowners. And it's actually like a buddy system. So we partner with them – make sure they're comfortable, make sure they understand the information and the process of becoming a homeowner. I'll make sure that she has a way here, if she needs assistance with her children, and things such as that. I'll be her buddy through the process of building her home."

I talked to Myles Odaniell and his 16-year-old son, Harrison, who was volunteering for the first time, helping to build 91 homes for 91 families in Jeff-Vander-Lou. The father and son were at first uncomfortable about being interviewed, but they warmed to the idea when I told them that the interview wasn't about them but about how people could benefit through their example. I asked Harrison how it felt to work with his father to help out the community. He leaned over and put an arm around his dad's shoulder.

"It actually feels really good," he said. "I've never been entirely involved in the community as much as I'd like to be, but my dad and his company have given me the opportunity to do so and I already feel wonderful about it."

"Hello, old chap, you got to work, hey?"

Tom wheeled suddenly and said:

"Why, it's you, Ben! I warn't noticing."

"Say—I'm going in a-swimming, I am. Don't you wish you could? But of course you'd druther work — wouldn't you? Course you would!"

Tom contemplated the boy a bit, and said:

"What do you call work?"

"Why, ain't that work?"

Tom resumed his whitewashing, and answered carelessly:

"Well, maybe it is, and maybe it ain't. All I know is, it suits Tom Sawyer."

"Oh come, now, you don't mean to let on that you like it?"

The brush continued to move.

"Like it? Well, I don't see why I oughtn't to like it. Does a boy get a chance to whitewash a fence every day?"

—*The Adventures of Tom Sawyer*, 1876, Chapter 2

As I made my way back to the river, I thought about my evening with the Jackson family and relived that joyful moment when we talked of their move to a new home in Jeff-Vander-Lou. I had looked at 7-year-old Ledra, who was making Spider-Man eyes with his fingers, and asked: "Ledra, when you see the pictures of the new house, what do they make you think of?" Taking his fingers away from his eyes, he had looked to his brother and then to his mother, as if to make sure it was OK for him to speak freely. "Being proud," he said, without any coaching. "Being proud and being free."

Turning to Alexander, I had asked what he thought about moving to the new house. "I feel that our new house is going to be big and cheerful," he said. We had been sitting around the kitchen table and I looked to the boys' mother, who had been grinning at the boys' answers, but her lips were quivering and she seemed on the verge of tears. Then, with a huge smile, she used her hands to simulate a rocket taking flight. "We're moving positive, I tell you," she said. "We're shooting for the stars."

————

It was nearly dark, a few nights after leaving St. Louis, when I paddled toward shore at Grand Tower, Ill. I made camp at the base of a ridge of low bluffs, draped the rain fly over my tent and hiked over the bluffs to an RV park, where I saw an elderly gentleman whom I took to be the proprietor. I inadvertently interrupted his conversation with a middle-aged couple in a Suburban parked outside the man's office. The old-timer and I shook hands, and I asked if I could pay to camp along the bank of the river. "I appreciate you asking, but there'll be no charge for you," he said. "You're on the river and we have a certain respect for that." The couple in the Suburban asked if I was a canoeist. When I said yes, the driver bellowed a greeting and asked if they could take me to dinner. I said I'd be delighted to accept their offer, and the couple got out of the vehicle and introduced themselves as Randy and Linda Elliot.

I shook their hands and Linda got back into the Suburban, continuing to converse with the proprietor. My new friend Randy led me back toward the bluffs, where we paused and looked out at the river. The water sparkled in the moonlight, bubbling and gurgling as it flowed past an island directly in front of us. Randy told me that the tall rock formation, which juts precipitously out of the river, is called Tower Rock, or Grand Tower, from which the nearby town takes its name. It has been a noteworthy landmark on the river for centuries, long before the French priest Jacques Marquette explored the Mississippi in 1673 and wrote that the island was "dreaded by the Savages," who believed it was the home of a man-devouring demon.

"I've lived on the river for 51 years," Randy said, still staring out at the rushing water. "That's how old I am. I'm 51 years old and I've lived along her shore, by choice, my entire life." That's a nanosecond, I thought, in the life of this ancient watercourse, formed a long time before any people were around to gawk at it, as Randy and I were doing on that splendid evening.

Randy asked about my journey, specifically whether I noticed any difference in paddling the river below St. Louis – beyond which there are no longer any locks and dams to maintain the depth of the navigation channel at a minimum of nine feet. I said that my first day out after leaving St. Louis was very windy and the water choppy, that I had trouble controlling my canoe and that I holed up on shore to await better weather.

"Above St. Louis, you've got a canal," Randy said. "Below St. Louis we've got a river. The river has got moods. Right now she's calm – but she can get wicked. Open those flood gates from the lakes and mix that with some serious rain and she'll turn nasty, she'll turn wicked. From here on out, there are no more dams, no artificial blockades. From here on out, my boy, you're looking at a river wild."

We stood for a long time, watching the river and the rising

moon. I felt as if I could have stood there all night, taking in the majesty of it all.

"What's your impression of the island?" Randy asked, breaking the silence and gesturing toward the Missouri shore. I had passed the towering rock earlier in search of a campsite, but its steep sides offered no place to pitch a tent. So I paddled back upriver with great difficulty to camp on the sandy embankment on the Illinois side.

"The place looks ancient and mysterious," I offered, to which Randy replied, "To be sure, it is both of those." He paused, and I knew that a story was coming on.

"In days gone by some folks called it Devil's Rock 'cause the Indians believed the island was evil, but its real name is Tower Rock," Randy said. "Early sailors would hoist their drinks to the place, in a celebration of making it past, in a sort of rite of passage. But don't let the beauty of the water fool you – the currents surrounding this stretch of river, in general, are treacherous. They say in the 1800s, a young couple were married right up on top of the island, but on their way back to shore the entire wedding party got sucked into a whirlpool and all but one drowned – the newlyweds and their priest, included."

Now the engines were stopped altogether, and we drifted with the current. Not that I could see the boat drift, for I could not, the stars being all gone by this time. This drifting was the dismalest work; it held one's heart still. Presently I discovered a blacker gloom than that which surrounded us. It was the head of the island. We were closing right down upon it. We entered its deeper shadow, and so imminent seemed the peril that I was likely to suffocate; and I had the strongest impulse to do SOMETHING, anything, to save the vessel. But still Mr. Bixby stood by his wheel, silent, intent as a cat, and all the pilots stood shoulder to shoulder at his back.

'She'll not make it!' somebody whispered.

The water grew shoaler and shoaler, by the leadsman's cries, till it was down to –

'Eight-and-a-half! ... E-i-g-h-t feet! ... E-i-g-h-t feet! ... Seven-and –'

Mr. Bixby said warningly through his speaking tube to the engineer –

'Stand by, now!'

'Aye-aye, sir!'

'Seven-and-a-half! Seven feet! Six-and –'

We touched bottom! Instantly Mr. Bixby set a lot of bells ringing, shouted through the tube, 'NOW, let her have it – every ounce you've got!' then to his partner, 'Put her hard down! snatch her! snatch her!' The boat rasped and ground her way through the sand, hung upon the apex of disaster a single tremendous instant, and then over she went! And such a shout as went up at Mr. Bixby's back never loosened the roof of a pilot-house before!

There was no more trouble after that. Mr. Bixby was a hero that night; and it was some little time, too, before his exploit ceased to be talked about by river men.

Fully to realize the marvelous precision required in laying the great steamer in her marks in that murky waste of water, one should know that not only must she pick her intricate way through snags and blind reefs, and then shave the head of the island so closely as to brush the overhanging foliage with her stern, but at one place she must pass almost within arm's reach of a sunken and invisible wreck that would snatch the hull timbers from under her if she should strike it, and destroy a quarter of a million dollars' worth of steam-boat and cargo in five minutes, and maybe a hundred and fifty human lives into the bargain.

The last remark I heard that night was a compliment to Mr. Bixby, uttered in soliloquy and with unction by one of our guests. He said—

'By the Shadow of Death, but he's a lightning pilot!'

—Life on the Mississippi, 1883, Chapter 7

I'd put in at Grand Tower hoping to find a hot meal, and that's exactly what I got. Randy and I headed back to the Suburban, and with his wife we drove slowly along the town's main street.

"There used to be only 10 families in this town," Randy said. "I was the former mayor. The current mayor, whose hand you shook earlier at the RV park along the river, is kin."

Randy could best be described as "wonderfully hillbilly," and I don't mean that as a slight. He and Linda were charming, authentic and deeply connected to the Mississippi and the people who live along her banks. He wore camouflage pants, and as we drove along, he talked of hunting. "Killed my first deer last season. Can you believe that?" he asked. "Fifty-one years of hunting and this was my very first deer." Linda wisecracked: "I've killed more than that with my SUV."

We pulled up at a convenience store and walked inside. As Randy and Linda exchanged greetings with the store's only other customer, I went to the buffalo wing counter and ordered a pizza and some wings. As we waited for the dinner to warm up, the three of us and the other customer took seats at a wooden table. I asked Randy if he'd ever seen hundreds of pelicans flying in formation, as I had witnessed north of the town. "I think we call them white turkeys," Randy quipped.

I got my to-go pizza and wings and we headed back to the RV park. I told the Elliots about my plans to stop at Cairo. "The town is half white and half black," Randy said. "Some parts are like a ghost town and some parts aren't safe. But I've been there and you'll find good people. It's a good town with a lot of history."

I thanked Randy and Linda for their hospitality and made my way down the hill to my campsite by the light of the Suburban's high beams. The moon rose full that night and provided plenty of light as I sat on my Coleman cooler and watched the river – pizza in one hand, buffalo wings in the other – all by myself.

I slept that night with the flaps of my tent open to the river. The gentle breeze wafting into my canvas shelter reminded me of a lullaby that my mother used to croon to me in ancient Gaelic. I didn't understand the words as a child, and I have yet to fathom the secrets of this magnificent river. But that didn't stop me from listening – then or now.

I slept with the storm shelter attached to the back of the tent so that I could deploy it in a hurry if a storm came up. It's a good thing I did, for nasty weather rolled in early that morning. Inside the tent, with the storm shelter draped overhead, I was dry and warm, but bursting with eagerness to get back on the Mississippi and make for Cairo. Even in a storm, I heard the river's call.

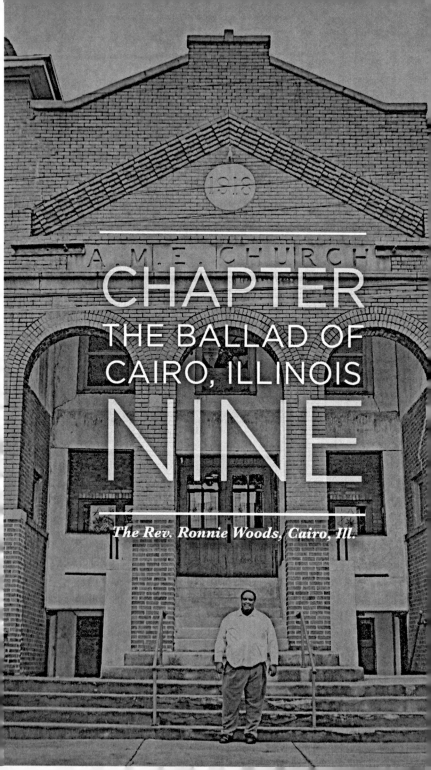

CHAPTER

THE BALLAD OF CAIRO, ILLINOIS

NINE

The Rev. Ronnie Woods, Cairo, Ill.

THE SKY SEEMED CURSED as the front rolled through, gray and black and crackling with electricity. I was a couple of days past Tower Rock, on the river and under assault by thunder and lightning. There was nowhere to put in, to get out of harm's way, to be dry and warm. As the pelting rain obscured the horizon, an Army Corps of Engineers patrol boat made several passes at my canoe, sweeping closer each time. The crewmen waved, apparently to see if I could wave back, to make sure I was alive.

Well, the second night a fog begun to come on, and we made for a towhead to tie to, for it wouldn't do to try to run in a fog; but when I paddled ahead in the canoe, with the line to make fast, there warn't anything but little saplings to tie to.

—*Adventures of Huckleberry Finn*, 1885, Chapter 5

After a while, the rain mercifully quit, the dark clouds passed and the sky opened up to bright sunshine. The weather became gloriously tranquil and the water became smooth again. I was wet to the bone and, even with the sun bearing down, I was a long way from being dry. So I paddled up to an island, stripped off my wet clothes and reached into my watertight Duluth bag for a set of dry duds.

Back on the Mississippi, I watched as a small group of motor yachts, which I had seen moored at Hoppie's Landing just below St. Louis, chugged past my canoe. The first two ignored me, but the third pulled directly alongside. The man at the vessel's elaborate wooden wheel was busy steering, but his first mate, whom I guessed to be his wife, came out on deck all smiles and shouted, "Is there anything we can do for you? Is there anything at all that you need?"

She sounded so sincere that I felt that I could have asked for anything – a glass of wine, a bit of cheese, cold beer, a respite from paddling aboard their cushy craft. But in truth I didn't need a thing. I was dry and warm and now back on schedule to make Cairo. The couple were pushing 60, but their yacht was called Young America, and it seemed that they had found the Fountain of Youth sought by Ponce de Leon. Amid laughter and good cheer, we exchanged contact information. They said they'd watch out for my CNN iReports and I promised to check out their blog. And then they were gone, the lot of us waving goodbye like old friends.

The good weather didn't last. As the sun dipped toward the western horizon, dark clouds gathered and threatened another storm. I thought of looking for a campsite and getting off the river. But I had arranged to meet the Rev. Kelly Cox in Cairo that evening, and the next morning I had an appointment with singer/songwriter Stace England, who in 2005 issued a CD of songs recounting the history of the town, "Greetings From Cairo." Stace had been one of my first contacts for this stretch of the river and was available for a meeting on only one day. So I paddled on.

Cairo, pronounced KAY-ro like the corn syrup rather than the city in Egypt, sits at the southern tip of Illinois at the confluence of the Ohio and Mississippi rivers and thus is prone to seasonal floods. The region of southern Illinois around Cairo to the north is called Little Egypt, partly because its flat, loamy landscape is reminiscent of the Nile River Delta. Cairo was founded in 1837 by the Cairo City & Canal Co. with grandiose notions of becoming a commercial hub at the intersection of the two mighty rivers.

Going into Cairo, we came near killing a steamboat which paid no attention to our whistle and then tried to cross our bows. By doing some strong backing, we saved him; which was a great loss, for he would have made good literature.

Cairo is a brisk town now; and is substantially built, and has a city look about it... Uncle Mumford says the libraries and Sunday-schools have done a good work in Cairo, as well as the brick masons. Cairo has a heavy railroad and river trade, and her situation at the junction of the two great rivers is so advantageous that she cannot well help prospering.

—*Life on the Mississippi*, 1883, Chapter 25

But Cairo is now enclosed by a series of levees and floodwalls, strengthened after the great flood of 1927, which effectively cut the town off from river commerce. Cairo has been in steep decline for decades and now is seen as a dying town. Its population peaked at 15,203 in the 1920 Census. Now, fewer than 3,000 people live there.

All that I had read about Cairo had been bad. It was said to be rife with crime and drugs, and the Alexander County sheriff's department recently had five of its seven patrol cars repossessed by a bank for nonpayment. Cairo had been featured in a Time magazine piece that showcased its downtown Main Street as the epitome of urban blight. On top of that, several of my friends and relatives contacted me in advance of my planned stop in Cairo and urged me not to set foot in the town without an armed escort.

I took their warnings seriously, but I figured that if I

couldn't find a positive story in Cairo, my feel-good safari would be a failure. Also, I reckoned that if I were being met by a minister and would be in his company during my stay, I'd be safe.

The first man of the cloth I had contacted in advance of my stop in Cairo was the Rev. Larry Potts, who told me that he would be unavailable the entire week and, besides, was too busy to meet me. That was probably a good thing. What I didn't know at the time was that Potts, now pastor of the Mighty Rivers Worship Center, had a checkered past. In January 1968, during a time when Cairo's blacks were waging a campaign for their civil rights, the segregationist minister clubbed to death an elderly black man whom he accused of trying to rape his wife. He was cleared by a coroner's jury and never went to trial. Later that year he helped form an all-white private school that he called Camelot.

I saw a man fling a lump of iron-ore at a slaveman in anger, for merely doing something awkwardly – as if that were a crime. It bounded from the man's skull, and the man fell and never spoke again. He was dead in an hour. I knew the man had a right to kill his slave if he wanted to, and yet it seemed a pitiful thing and somehow wrong, though why wrong I was not deep enough to explain if I had been asked to do it. Nobody in the village approved of that murder, but of course no one said much about it.

—*Following the Equator,* 1897, Chapter 38

On a tip from Stace England, I had contacted the Cairo
Public Library and had a delightful conversation with the
librarian. When I told her I hoped to interview a clergyman
in Cairo, she provided the name of the Rev. Cox, a United
Methodist pastor, and suggested that he'd be glad to put me up.
The Rev. Cox, she told me, was known throughout Cairo
for the chili he dispenses at an annual event on his front
verandah. "Everybody just loves the Rev. Cox's chili," she said.
"He serves it with a smile and he serves it all night long."
He sounded like a guy I'd like to meet, so I called him on my
cellphone to arrange a meeting. Our rendezvous was set for 7
o'clock that evening on the levee at Cairo, but I didn't know
at the time of our phone talk what an ordeal it would be to
make that meeting.

As I approached Cairo, I came to a big bridge and thought
that I couldn't be far from the Mississippi's meeting with the
Ohio. I shot some celebratory video because the confluence
with the Ohio River is considered the dividing point between
the Upper Mississippi and the Lower Mississippi. It was the
symbolic halfway point of my journey and I was still alive
to tell the tale – at least the first half. But that bridge, which
carries the traffic of Interstate 57 across the Mississippi
between Illinois and Missouri, turned out to be the first of
two bridges just upriver from the confluence. By the time
I paddled to the second bridge, the one for U.S. 60 and U.S.
62, the sun had gone down and a layer of fog denied any
hope of moonlight.

We talked about Cairo, and wondered whether we would know it when we got to it. I said likely we wouldn't, because I had heard say there warn't but about a dozen houses there, and if they didn't happen to have them lit up, how was we going to know we was passing a town? Jim said if the two big rivers joined together there, that would show. But I said maybe we might think we was passing the foot of an island and coming into the same old river again. That disturbed Jim – and me too. So the question was, what to do? I said, paddle ashore the first time a light showed, and tell them pap was behind, coming along with a trading-scow, and was a green hand at the business, and wanted to know how far it was to Cairo. Jim thought it was a good idea, so we took a smoke on it and waited.

There warn't nothing to do now but to look out sharp for the town, and not pass it without seeing it. He said he'd be mighty sure to see it, because he'd be a free man the minute he seen it, but if he missed it he'd be in a slave country again and no more show for freedom. Every little while he jumps up and says:

"Dah she is?"

—*Adventures of Huckleberry Finn*, 1885, Chapter 16

It was now 7 p.m., the appointed hour of my meeting with the Rev. Cox. I had hoped there would be a safe place to meet along the Mississippi. But Cairo faces the Ohio River and the levee along the front of the town offered the best spot to land a canoe. I was thus faced with the daunting challenge of navigating the turbulent water at the confluence and then paddling a handful of miles upstream on the Ohio River. It was nearly pitch dark as I rounded the sandy tip of land at the confluence and headed up the Ohio. This was a different, unfamiliar river, and I was fighting the raging current. I could see a large bridge just upstream from the confluence and thought that my goal, the town's boat ramp, was a bit beyond that.

I couldn't telephone the reverend just then because I was preoccupied with controlling my canoe and trying to propel it upstream. Forty minutes later, he called me. He said he was so concerned for my safety that he had summoned a sheriff's deputy. I heard him mutter "Sweet Jesus!" and the admonishment "Do you have any idea how dangerous this is?" He passed the phone to the deputy, who also began to reprimand me. I interrupted him and shouted into my cellphone: "How far is it to the hole in the levee past the bridge on the Ohio I see directly ahead of me?!" He shouted back: "About a mile or two, maybe two and a half miles. Watch out for the construction tows along the banks of the town – they're doing construction!"

I strapped a headlamp to my forehead and put my lantern at the prow of the canoe. Other than my own lights, there was no illumination to be seen except for the bridge and a few lights along the Cairo side of the Ohio River.

"We's safe, Huck, we's safe! Jump up and crack yo' heels! Dat's de good ole Cairo at las', I jis knows it!"

—*Adventures of Huckleberry Finn*, 1885, Chapter 16

I paddled stronger than I'd ever paddled. I was in a fight for my life, but I couldn't let myself think in those terms. I'd been trying to propel myself up the Ohio for more than an hour, and I realized that I was no closer to that damned bridge than I had been when I'd spoken with the reverend and the deputy 20 minutes before. I shined my headlamp onto the dark water and saw that it was running extremely fast – directly against me. The lights on the bridge were far in the distance, and through the fog I could just make them out. They blinked green and red, apparently marking the channel under the bridge. I couldn't see any traffic in the middle of the river because of the fog, but I could hear the pounding engines of towboats as they pushed past me with their barges. I became acutely aware that if I couldn't see them, they certainly couldn't see me.

Fortunately, the Cairo side of the river was relatively free of traffic. But I could make out some moving lights whose purpose I couldn't fathom. The fog was so thick that I couldn't see what the lights were attached to. At first I thought they might be on a boat coming to rescue me, but then I realized that that was a false hope.

"Maybe we went by Cairo in the fog that night."

He says:

"Doan' le's talk about it, Huck. Po' niggers can't have no luck. I awluz 'spected dat rattlesnake-skin warn't done wid its work."

"I wish I'd never seen that snake-skin, Jim – I do wish I'd never laid eyes on it."

"It ain't yo' fault, Huck; you didn' know. Don't you blame yo'self 'bout it."

When it was daylight, here was the clear Ohio water inshore, sure enough, and outside was the old regular Muddy! So it was all up with Cairo.

—*Adventures of Huckleberry Finn*, 1885, Chapter 16

The lights would rise up from water level to what appeared to be an impossible height, rotate from side to side and then perform what looked like a somersault. I guessed they must be attached to a crane on one of the construction boats that the deputy warned me about. When one of these monsters got too close to me I took the lantern from the bow of my canoe and held it high in the air. But every time I did this, the canoe would drift backward, costing me whatever precious progress I'd made. At long last, I made my way closer to the levee wall, but I saw that it was lined with moored barges. I dared not get too close to the barges because I knew that the swift current rushing past these behemoths could suck me under one of them.

The barges had lights strung on their hulls, and I could make out the names of the companies that owned them painted on the sides. As I paddled, I measured my forward progress by each letter I passed – a few inches with each stroke.

That gave me hope. "Keep going, you're going to make it," I said to myself over and over. I finally made it to the bridge and now had to look for the gap in the levee that the deputy told me about.

Those construction tows, with their cranes swinging about, were now closer. In one too-close encounter, a captain with a bullhorn barked out something like: "Are you tryin' to kill yourself? Do you have a death wish? Do you know what you're doing is ASININE to the greatest possible degree?" At least that's what I think he said. To be honest, I can't remember his exact words, but I knew by the way he screamed it that I was in real danger. All I could do was scream back: "How far to the boat ramp? How far to the hole in the Cairo levee wall?" To which the captain shouted a reply: "Look to the shore, you idiot! You're already there!"

I looked to the left as my canoe rode the wake of the construction tow – a stomach-churning upward thrust followed by a sharp dip – and through the fog I saw a small group of people who had gathered, apparently, to see whether I lived or died. They waved as I neared the boat ramp and I saw among them a short, pot-bellied man with a long white beard. I knew immediately that it was the Rev. Kelly Cox.

I hadn't asked on the phone whether he was white or African-American. It didn't matter. But I had assumed he was black, and I was wrong. I landed the canoe and walked up to meet him, a bit unsteady on my feet. "Good Lord!

Are you CRAZY?!" he called out as I approached. We shook hands, and he asked, "Is the story really worth THIS?" To which I laughed and replied: "Is it worth the story of Cairo? Absolutely!"

We drove through the gap in the town's massive levee wall and along Main Street. It looked as if a war had been fought there and that the opposing armies had now decamped. There were gaping holes in the walls and roofs of what had once been downtown commercial buildings. Others were sagging or collapsed into piles of rubble. But the voices all around me in the pastor's car were upbeat and hopeful. They spoke of townsfolk banding together, of projects under way, of making a stand. Clearly, it seemed, something had to be done because the situation couldn't get much worse.

When I awoke the next morning, the sun was already high in the sky. I was sure that the muscles in my back, arms and shoulders would be screaming for Advil. But the human body is a remarkably resilient machine. The night's rest under the reverend's roof made me feel whole again, and I felt fine. It was my first day in town and I was eager to see it all.

The Rev. Cox and I set out on our tour on foot and I asked if it was safe to walk about Cairo, considering all I had heard about the town. "I could sleep on this street and I'd feel perfectly safe," he said. "I've never had an incident, not one unfortunate turn of events, in all my years here."

We walked up and down several streets and ended up

a couple of blocks off Main Street at the Nu Diner, an eatery that has been in continual operation for five decades. The joint teemed with old-timers, the wise old souls of the town, seated in circular booths, laughing and chewing and giving the waitress a healthy dose of sass. Having delivered me safely indoors, the reverend excused himself, saying he had parishioners to attend to. So I bade farewell and went to one of the diner's booths to meet up with singer/songwriter Stace England.

Stace and his band, The Salt Kings, have used their music to tell the story of what he calls "the most fascinating town in America, bar none." Their 2005 CD, "Greetings From Cairo," traces the town's history "from 1858 to the present through the Civil War, lynchings, the blues years, civil rights struggles and spectacular decline," says the band's website. One song on the album is called "The North Starts in Cairo," a reference to the town's location on the Ohio River, which once roughly divided the slave states of the South and free states in the North.

"Back when blacks were traveling by bus from the South, they were separated by a curtain from the white riders," Stace said as we talked at the Nu Diner, speaking of America's time of racial segregation. "They could take that curtain down in Cairo, because the North started here. So you can imagine people who had lived with segregation their entire lives getting into the land of opportunity – a very dramatic thing."

But the land of opportunity, or "the Promised Land,"

as runaway slaves called it, was not full of promise for all citizens. As I sat in the diner with Stace, I wondered what Huck Finn's raft mate, the slave Jim, would think if he could visit Cairo now.

Are we a nation still divided by race? What lessons have we learned from the Civil War, Reconstruction, the Jim Crow era, the civil rights movement and, most recently, the election of our first black president?

I looked to the far side of the café, where a solitary black customer was holding court at the head of a table of white old-timers, and I was intrigued. "That's Preston Ewing," Stace said. "He helped me a great deal with my research for my album. Preston was the president of the local NAACP in the late '60s, is the city treasurer and unofficial town historian today."

Stace and I had paid our tab and we intercepted Ewing as he was about to leave the diner. He shook my hand slowly, with the inquisitive look of a man who can read people. He had obviously seen a great deal in his life, and, as a historian, had taken note. But when I asked him about his own experiences and how the town had dealt with the civil rights movement, he laughed off his own role and turned the discussion back to the town. "Before you can capture a glimpse of Cairo's future, you've most certainly got to understand its past," he said.

I explained to him my search for positive American stories and asked for an interview. Come by my office later on this afternoon," he said, "and I'll put a packet of information into your hands, detailing what we've been through, of who we are."

Stace had his guitar with him as we walked back to Main Street. When we reached the dilapidated thoroughfare, I shot video of him singing and playing his guitar as he strode down the middle of the street, in the middle of the day, with almost no one around to watch. "The glory days are gone, leaving only a trace," Stace sang as he strummed. "But each time another building falls down, a garden could grow in its place. Hold on, hold on, and open up your heart. We can build together, or keep watching things fall apart."

Rain began to fall, and the sad scene looked even sadder. But we kept right at it, walking and singing and recording video.

A couple of blocks from Main, just inside the levee wall along the Ohio River, Stace showed me the hulk of a once-grand hotel that now stood as silent testimony to Cairo's decline. Next to the hotel was a blues club that now sang its own version of the blues. Tucked just under a nearby levee road was a recently discovered series of round brick tunnels, which historians believe was part of the Underground Railroad. Runaway slaves like Jim in *Huckleberry Finn* would have been spirited off the river into the hands of white abolitionists and free blacks and dispatched to other places of refuge on their journey further north. Here was tangible evidence that whites and blacks had once stood together in the cause of freedom.

Stace suggested that we stop in at the Alexander County

Courthouse to meet with the county's first African-American circuit clerk, Bishop Paul Jones.

Bishop Jones looked right at home in his role as county clerk. He spoke at length about the town's history, recorded in volumes labeled year by year on the shelves of his antiquated office. "Cairo was the safe-haven point for slaves leaving the South," he said. "If you made it to Cairo and crossed the Ohio River, then you could consider yourself to be on somewhat free territory."

> *Both of these river towns have been retired to the country by that cut-off. A cut-off plays havoc with boundary lines and jurisdictions: for instance, a man is living in the State of Mississippi to-day, a cut-off occurs to-night, and to-morrow the man finds himself and his land over on the other side of the river, within the boundaries and subject to the laws of the State of Louisiana! Such a thing, happening in the upper river in the old times, could have transferred a slave from Missouri to Illinois and made a free man of him.*

—*Life on the Mississippi*, 1885, Chapter 1

Jones was originally from Kentucky on the other side of the Ohio River, but he had lived in Cairo for several decades. He was a font of knowledge on the town's history, and he looked like a professor with his spectacles and salt-and-pepper beard. I asked about the church's role in the Civil War era. He leaned back in his chair, with his hands clasped behind his head, and I knew we were in for an interesting tale.

"There was a white minister by the name of J.S. Manning who took up residence here, back during the time of the Civil War," Bishop Jones said. "The reason for him coming to this area was on account of a number of runaway slaves who were coming back with the soldiers that had barracks over on the west end of Cairo, up near the levee. They were coming back, and because they were considered chattel and not considered to be human beings, they were not allowed to learn how to read and write.

"So Minister Manning opened up a church school here and started teaching black men how to read and write and become ministers of the gospel," the bishop went on.

"And when they became ministers of the gospel they crossed over the Ohio River and went on over into Kentucky, Indiana, Pennsylvania, Virginia, West Virginia and Maryland. They went to North Carolina, to Mississippi, to Arkansas, Louisiana and some parts of Texas. They went on to those places and began to preach the gospel and to set up churches. But it all started here," he said with a note of pride.

"Our church is the parent church of many Freewill Baptist Churches that are still in existence today, starting way back during the days of the Civil War. These churches would become involved, as many churches were, with the Underground Railroad in this area. As I say, as many churches were because they were considered a safe-haven place and a lot of ministers that did not believe in the slavery concept would always try to help someone out on the run."

Then the preacher begun to preach, and begun in earnest, too; and went weaving first to one side of the platform and then the other, and then a-leaning down over the front of it, with his arms and his body going all the time, and shouting his words out with all his might; and every now and then he would hold up his Bible and spread it open, and kind of pass it around this way and that, shouting, "It's the brazen serpent in the wilderness! Look upon it and live!" And people would shout out, "Glory!–A-a-men!" And so he went on, and the people groaning and crying and saying amen..."

—*Adventures of Huckleberry Finn*, 1885, Chapter 20

The town's legacy as a place of refuge before, during and just after the Civil War was in sharp contrast to its role a century later as a flashpoint in the civil rights movement.

What sparked the violence in Cairo was the death of 19-year-old Army Pfc. Robert L. Hunt Jr. He was found hanged with an undershirt, said to be his own, and severely beaten in the city jail in the early hours of July 16, 1967. He had been a passenger in a car stopped by Cairo police for having a defective taillight and arrested for being verbally abusive. Hunt's death led to four days of fires and shootings. Two months later, a coroner's inquest ruled Hunt's death a suicide, despite evidence of a beating and Hunt's friends saying he wasn't wearing an undershirt the night of his arrest. Later, the U.S. Commission on Civil Rights issued a report titled "Cairo: A Symbol of Racial Polarization," followed by another,

"Cairo: Racism at Floodtide."

For more insight on the history of race relations in Cairo, I telephoned the Rev. Ronnie Woods, a teacher and former football coach at Cairo Junior/Senior High School. It seemed that everyone I met in Cairo was a minister of some sort. Woods presided over the local A.M.E. Church.

At the front door of the school, I met the principal, and he called out, "Ronnie!" My first glimpse of the Rev. Woods told me why he had been a football coach. He was immense, larger than life, all smiles. His joviality and enthusiasm for the job seemed to infect the other teachers – black and white, male and female – that he introduced me to as we strolled about the school.

Ronnie showed me the classroom where he taught shop and photos of his students on the wall. He told me that he and his students helped keep the school functioning. Any time something broke in the school – a slide projector, a radio, a desk – he would have it delivered to his class and his students would fiddle around with it and make it right again.

Having been warned beforehand that Cairo was a town on the skids and that it would be tough to find anything positive in such a place, I was delighted by what I saw at Cairo Junior/Senior High School. Instead of the teachers being sullen and jaded, I found that they seemed cheerful, competent and passionate about their work.

I asked Ronnie what he remembered of the civil rights struggle in Cairo and how it had shaped him.

"In 1966," he began, "when I was at Washington Grade School, which was an all-black school, I was a sixth-grader. My first year of integration was the seventh grade. Before that I had never gone to school with white kids. So as we went on and we integrated up at the Cairo Junior High, you know, it was interesting. I looked at it as, OK, this is going to be, different. It was going to be a change. And sometimes change is scary. But with all the other things that were going on in the community at the time, your awareness was heightened of the differences. But we learned how to bridge those differences and come together. And that was the cool thing about the people I grew up with. As a seventh-grader, I had a front-row seat in watching history."

As the Rev. Larry Potts was unavailable for comment, I spent the next few days tying up loose ends with Bishop Jones, the Revs. Woods and Cox, Preston Ewing and Judson Childs, the town's first African-American mayor.

What I gleaned during my visit to Cairo was an understanding of how it could be if the people I met had their way. Those who have chosen to stay here do so because they have hope for their community.

In parting, Ronnie Woods recounted a surprising tale about the Rev. Potts, whose long-ago killing of a black man divided the community. He said that Potts had come knocking on the door of Woods' A.M.E. Church, which had been a launch pad for marches and protests four decades previously. Potts was accompanied by members of his white congregation who toted cans of paint and brushes. They had come to paint the A.M.E. Church. Ronnie said he guessed they had come, without stating so directly, to apologize for their pastor's brutal attack in 1968.

I asked Ronnie what he thought about the Potts's sign of contrition. He pondered for a while, displayed his trademark smile, and said:

"We have the opportunity to pull together as a nation and as a community because we understand being separate doesn't work. And it doesn't work for anybody. We can't grow as a nation. We couldn't grow as a community. Because we were fighting a war, we were fighting issues that were not allowing us to be able to come together and grow. We needed each other. And now, especially with the economic situations that we have, we desperately need each other. If we stay divided in our camps, all we're going to do is fall. And this nation will fall. We need each other desperately. So the lessons that we learned here, after all the struggles, everything that went on – is that we need each other in order to grow. And we can't grow, in this community, without each other. And I think we've learned that."

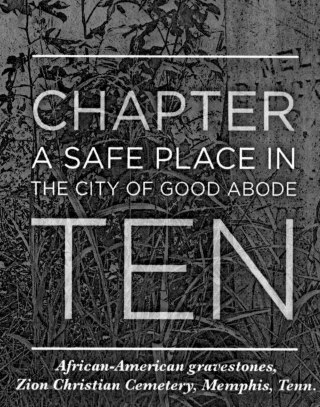

CHAPTER

A SAFE PLACE IN
THE CITY OF GOOD ABODE

TEN

*African-American gravestones,
Zion Christian Cemetery, Memphis, Tenn.*

FROM THE MOMENT I spotted it, the shimmering patch of sand was calling my name. It often happened this way. I'd paddle for hours without seeing a suitable spot to camp, and then, just in time, in concert with the setting sun, I'd find sanctuary – at least for that night. I consulted my river map and identified the place as Moore Island. Was it named for one of my distant forbearers? Probably not, but I took comfort – misplaced comfort as events transpired – to be camping on an island that bore my name.

After its meeting with the Ohio, the Mississippi booms

along with extra force, as if sensing that its course to the sea is no longer constrained by locks and dams. As I cut to the left with deep strokes and pointed my canoe at the towhead, a huge eddy blocked my way. You hear the burble and gurgle of these beasts before you see them, and then your survival instinct kicks in. The debris of five days' rain – logs, branches, Styrofoam, plastic bottles and other river trash – was caught up in this muddy maelstrom that was trying to keep me from my campsite.

> *The current tore through there like a mill-race, and the boat darted through like a telegram. The passage was made in half a minute; then we were in a wide place where noble vast eddies swept grandly round and round in shoal water, and I wondered what they would do with the little boat. They did as they pleased with her.*

> —*Following the Equator*, 1897, Chapter 32

I paddled hard and fast to avoid the eddy and got caught momentarily on its outer edge. But that fleeting encounter spun the canoe back on course to the towhead and deposited me on the sandbar's northern tip.

It wasn't much of an island, but it would certainly do. My general rule for camping on islands was to tie the canoe to a stout tree and pitch the tent on the highest ground I could find. But the high ground at the center of Moore's Island was thick with brush and trees. So I made camp on the patch of sand at the island's northern end, which had caught my eye upriver. I had a feeling of foreboding and claustrophobia as I settled into the tent, only a few feet from the water's edge.

Indeed, the Island Wilderness is the very home of romance and dreams and mystery. The loneliness, the solemnity, the beauty, and the deep repose of this wilderness have a charm which is all their own...

—*Following the Equator,* 1897, Chapter

As towboats and their barges passed in the night, the beams of their searchlights sometimes scanned the island, creating eerie silhouettes on the inner walls of the tent. The small waves created by the boats' wakes lapped at the edges of the sandbar and made a comforting sound. By this stage of my trip, I felt that the towboats were my friends in the night, their mournful horns as familiar as the night calls of birds. But I was gripped by a sense of unease about this night and this place.

I loaded and cocked my Snake Charmer shotgun, ready to dispense mayhem if uninvited visitors came calling. Out here in the wild, I had become hardened in a way that I both loved and abhorred. I felt confident, yet fearful, as I dozed fitfully during the first couple hours, alert to the sounds of the night.

The constant awakening was torment, and my inner voice screamed "Danger!" I unzipped the flaps of my tent and shined my light outside. The Mississippi was on the rise, her water only inches from my front door.

I dragged the Andrea to higher ground and lashed her

again to a sturdy cottonwood. I rushed back and grabbed my bags, took down my tent and then struggled through the dense underbrush to the highest point on the island. But even that spot afforded only a few more feet of elevation. From there, I had no view of the river, only the company of the cottonwoods that shivered and swayed in what turned out to be a howler of a storm. Back in my tent I was mesmerized by the shadows dancing on the sides of the canvas, cast by the light of my hurricane lantern hanging in a tree just overhead.

After a few more hours of sporadic sleep, I again peered out from my tent and, to my alarm, found the river perilously close. The Mississippi lapped at my shins as it evicted me from the island. I snatched down the tent, threw all my gear into the canoe, grabbed the lantern from the tree and was off into the rising river. I floated for a few minutes amid the trees on my fast-submerging island before being hit by the full force of the flood tide.

Out on the dark river, I paddled furiously in the raging water, on the lookout for floating trees and the monster towboats that ply the Lower Mississippi. The rain beat down and the wind kept trying to push me off course. Maybe for the first time during this trip, I seriously questioned my sanity. The Mississippi had risen about five feet in the past few hours, and it was hard not to take it personally.

I held tight to my paddles and focused on the long haul. At first light, I scanned the riverbanks for a suitable place to pull off. I spotted a boat ramp on the Missouri side of the river across from Hickman, Ky., and made directly for it. After hauling my canoe a safe distance up the ramp, I collapsed on the ground and lay there in the rain a long while, thanking my lucky stars that I was alive.

The blast of a horn roused me from my reverie and I saw that the ramp was the landing for a private ferry, which was now bearing down on me. I dragged the canoe off to the side and stood there like a fool, waving at the ferry skipper. To my surprise, he waved back.

Edward Fuller was a jovial young soul who had gotten his ferry operator's license only a season or two back. He was solidly built and must have been in his early 20s. He had been raised on the river and was intimately familiar with her ways. He talked briefly of the river's mercurial personality and the knowledge required to become a ferryboat captain. Then the focus of the conversation shifted to me. He warned me of the hazards on the river between Hickman and Memphis, and with a dead-serious look, he offered some ominous words about my mode of transport. Pointing to a bend just across the river near Hickman, he said gigantic eddies often form there and that they can spin full-sized boats "something silly."

"I'm not sure if I should call you crazy – or praise you," Fuller said.

I looked out at the choppy water and, taking his words to heart, thought about riding the ferry over to Hickman to take a respite from this madness. But as we continued to talk, I found myself defending the journey and my choice of a canoe as the means of doing it. And then the unexpected occurred. The next time I looked out at the river, I saw, to my astonishment, that the wind had died down and the surface was as smooth as glass. Just like that! The river was still running fast, but there wasn't a wave in sight. I took it as a sign. I smiled at my new friend, gestured toward the river and said, "Well, that's it. It looks as if I'm going to expedition forth after all."

Fuller gave me a bright orange rain slicker, some snacks and extra water and a dose of friendly advice. "Hug the Missouri side," he said. "Get completely off the river when a monster barge approaches, but do not step foot onto Island No. 8. It's a hunting island where they'll shoot you on sight."

As luck would have it, I had to make two emergency stops on Island No. 8, as two monster towboats, one after the other, pushed their barges along the same course that I was taking. Given a choice of death by towboat or death by hunter, I decided to take my chances with the hunters. But it was a close call. Fuller had warned me, "Hunters down here don't care about Christmas. For them, it's all about the start of hunting season. They stock that island with deer, and if you land on their island without an invite, they'll think you're a poacher, and they'll shoot you."

Just before landing the first time, I spotted a buck in the

thick of the island's old-growth trees, but he scampered out of sight the moment he saw me. I instinctively took cover behind an outcropping of rocks, thankful that the buck's eyes – I hoped – were the only ones that had seen me.

Back on the river, the current was so swift that at times, close to the shore, the foliage was just a swirl of green and brown. The river continued to rise and before long it was rare to see an island with any exposed sand. Most were submerged, with only the tops of their trees sticking out of the water. There was nothing easy about this stretch of the trip. I realized that I was quite literally fighting to stay alive to tell the stories I had set out to tell.

The rain returned, in scattered showers at first, and then in a torrent. Cold and soaked to the skin, I snaked-danced through the Mississippi's twists and turns, dodging the eddies and running for shore at the sound of a towboat. But at last I made it to Memphis, tired, dirty and exhausted.

Sleep came easy that night.

————

My time as an itinerant canoeist on the Mississippi had given me some inkling of what it must be like to be homeless: sleeping in a different place most nights, at the mercy of the elements, thankful for the kindness of strangers. So I felt some empathy as I plunged into the story that I wanted to tell in Memphis: Youth Villages, safe havens for the city's abused, homeless and runaway children. Nevertheless, I could hardly imagine what it must feel like for a kid to be thrust out of a home, separated from family, trying to survive in an indifferent world.

> *He got to hanging around the widow's too much and so she told him at last that if he didn't quit using around there she would make trouble for him. Well, wasn't he mad? He said he would show who was Huck Finn's boss. So he watched out for me one day in the spring, and catched me, and took me up the river about three mile in a skiff, and crossed over to the Illinois shore where it was woody and there warn't no houses but an old log hut in a place where the timber was so thick you couldn't find it if you didn't know where it was.*

> *He kept me with him all the time, and I never got a chance to run off. We lived in that old cabin, and he always locked the door and put the key under his head nights. He had a gun which he had stole, I reckon, and we fished and hunted, and that was what we lived on. Every little while he locked me in and went down to the store, three miles, to the ferry, and traded fish and game for whisky, and fetched it home and got drunk and had a good time, and licked me.*

—*Adventures of Huckleberry Finn*, 1885, Chapter 6

I reached out to Meagan Holgan, volunteer coordinator for Youth Villages, a private, nonprofit organization founded in Memphis in 1986 to help "emotionally and behaviorally troubled children and their families," according to its website.

Youth Villages started out helping a handful of kids in Memphis and now provides services each year to more than 18,000 children and families from 20 states and the District of Columbia. It offers residential treatment, in-home counseling, foster care, adoption and transitional living services. Halloween was not far away, and I accepted Meagan's invitation to join her and the kids as they carved pumpkins at an arts and crafts night.

Memphis is probably best known for Graceland, Elvis Presley's tacky mansion; the blues bars on Beale Street; the stainless steel pyramid on the river; the triple-A affiliate of the St. Louis Cardinals, the Memphis Redbirds; and the Lorraine Motel, where Martin Luther King Jr. was assassinated in 1968. It was a thriving entrepot for slaves and cotton before the Civil War, and, in the first half of the 20th century, fortunes were made in lumber, cotton and mules. Lately, like a lot of cities along the river, it wore all the scars of hard times: crime, unemployment and general decay. But no matter how hard the times, there always seem to be people and organizations ready to lend a hand – groups such as Youth Villages, reaching out to children caught up in situations not of their own making.

All Offal Court was just such another hive as Canty's house. Drunkenness, riot, and brawling were the order there, every night and nearly all night long. Broken heads were as common as hunger in that place. Yet little Tom was not unhappy. He had a hard time of it, but did not know it. It was the sort of time that all the Offal

Court boys had, therefore he supposed it was the correct and comfortable thing. When he came home empty-handed at night, he knew his father would curse him and thrash him first, and that when he was done the awful grandmother would do it all over again and improve on it; and that away in the night his starving mother would slip to him stealthily with any miserable scrap of crust she had been able to save for him by going hungry herself, notwithstanding she was often caught in that sort of treason and soundly beaten for it by her husband.

—*The Prince and the Pauper,* 1882, Chapter 2

The Youth Villages' Tudor-style group home, where the pumpkin-carving party was held, had the look and feel of a well-tended house in suburbia. I entered to the sound of laughter and the aroma of roasting pumpkin seeds. The teenaged boys who lived here were served by a steady rotation of volunteer counselors from the local charity Volunteer Mid-South. Volunteers had gathered this brisk September evening to help inject a bit of normality into the boys' lives – carving pumpkins, as kids across America do at this time of year.

Kim Motschman took a break from roasting pumpkin seeds to explain. "Most of the projects are types of mentoring," she said, "presenting good role models, because a lot of times the projects we'll do, on a monthly basis, are projects the kids don't normally get to do. We'll go and play ball games outside or have cookouts. We'll do lots of arts and crafts – things of that nature."

Kim said she's touched by the relationship that the kids and the volunteers develop over time. "Even though they may be a bit more difficult because they've had more difficult lives than a lot of us," she went on, "they've really grown attached and enjoy us coming."

Choking back tears, she recalled that she missed a month or two of volunteering some time back and that the kids were full of concern and questions when she returned. "We all feel very blessed to have these relationships," she said. "I'm gettin' all teary. That's OK."

In the dining room, the kids' smiles mimicked those they were carving on the pumpkins. One boy held his pumpkin beside his face, posing like a pair of brothers in a family snapshot. As I watched another boy carve intricate designs on his pumpkin, I noticed that one of his arms was covered with equally intricate tattoos. Yes, they were just kids, but these boys had come from hard lives on the streets.

"A lot of the children that we work with have come from unstable backgrounds," Meagan Holgan said. "Most of them we find have been abused in some way, whether that's emotional abuse, physical abuse, or sexual abuse.

"A lot of them," she said, "come from homes where there's not a lot of structure … Maybe they didn't have a positive adult role model to show them a positive way of behaving in the community. So the children here, because of that environment they've grown up in, have sometimes made some poor decisions that have led to them being unsafe in the community – which is why we bring them here to help work with their behaviors.

"We don't just take children out of their community and fix them," she said. "We bring children to our campuses; we involve parents. Most of our children have parental visitation at least once a month, if not more. When the parents visit the kids, they're also participating in family therapy."

Meagan stressed that children are best raised in families that live in communities, not by institutions. So Youth Villages gets the community involved to help the child get back to normal family life.

"As the child is getting ready to transition back home," Meagan said, "we put counselors in the home to work with mom and dad or grandpa, grandma, auntie, uncle – anyone the child is going to be interacting with. And they get the community involved to help prepare the home for that child to come back.

"That's really why I feel that Youth Villages is so successful with the children that we serve. We don't focus solely on the individual. … We focus on the whole ecosystem that that child is coming from."

I tried to strike up a conversation with the boy with the tattooed arm. He tried to speak, but the words didn't come out. During that awkward moment, the boy's friend, who had been watching, stepped up, smiled, and said he would like to speak.

"My name is Sean," he said, filling in for his shy friend. "I'm 16. I'm at Poplar Group Home at Youth Villages. I've been here for two years – a little over. I've made a lot of improvement. I just want to say I've been here long enough and I'm ready to go home."

He offered kind words for "the great volunteers Memphis has."

"You know, just to realize that people are out here to help us," he said, "not just people that will harm us."

As Sean spoke, police cars raced down the street outside, sirens blaring. It was a reminder of the rough lives these boys had come from and how fortunate they were to have found a place of refuge. When the sound of the sirens faded away, Sean spoke about his mentors.

"The mentoring program is important because there's kids that need help and there's kids that need older brothers and sisters that haven't had them in the past," he said. "My mentor is sort of like an older brother/father for me because my father was actually never there. So, I look up to him."

I asked Sean what advice he'd give to other kids from troubled families. He thought for a moment and said: "Well, all I got to say is there are people out there that like to help. Don't try to hide – try to trust people – because when you're down and lonely there's always someone you can talk to. Don't just try to hide your feelings."

I thanked the boys, their counselors and the volunteers

as I got ready to leave. Earlier, I had asked a night counselor, a lovely young woman named Tiffany Dickerson, what she thought about her work with Youth Villages. The night was crisp and clear as I walked back to the city center, and Tiffany's answer reflected my own feelings.

"When you leave here you've got that warm feeling in your heart," she had said. "You just feel really warm on the inside. You've helped this child – because these children, some days they've got their ups and some days they've got their downs, but when you've talked to the child at the end of the evening, you feel more comfortable with yourself knowing that they feel good about everything. And my inspiration? I love helping them. It puts a smile on my face because it puts a smile on their face."

In his autobiographical book Life on the Mississippi, Mark Twain called Memphis the "Good Samaritan city" because of the care given by its physicians and other residents to his younger brother Henry and other victims of a boiler explosion aboard the steamboat Pennsylvania in 1858.

The name still rings true.

————

When Memphis was founded in 1819 on a high bluff overlooking the Mississippi River, one of the city fathers, John Overton, predicted that it would become one of the great cities of the United States and could rival its Egyptian namesake on the Nile River. Memphis, as the name came down to us through ancient Egyptian and Greek, translates roughly as "the place of good abode." Memphis, Tenn., adopted that description as its own and calls itself "the city of good abode."

During my sojourn in Memphis, I became enchanted with its downtown – the trolleys, the barbecue, the riverfront, the music, the history. Staying in a comfortable hotel didn't seem quite right. It was as if I were breaking the unwritten code of the river rat. I presented quite a spectacle that first night when I pitched up at the reception desk with a canoe, bulging river bags, a plastic cooler, paddles and Foreign Legion hat. Nearly everyone in the lobby offered some comment. But it was the hotel staff that most appreciated the fact that I was canoeing the river. They spirited away my river-weathered clothes for a free wash and press and found a secure spot for my canoe in the courtyard out back. All done with a smile!

I had chosen these digs because of the location – in the center of downtown, close to the Mississippi, perched just above the city's historic cobblestone streets. Through the open windows of my room, I could take in the sights, sounds and smells of the city. Outside, I could thrust myself immediately into its daily life: panhandling down-and-outers, men in business suits, police cars – all accompanied by the ding, ding, ding of the streetcar bells.

A thriving place is the Good Samaritan City of the Mississippi: has a great wholesale jobbing trade; foundries, machine shops; and manufactories of wagons, carriages, and cotton-seed oil; and is shortly to have cotton mills and elevators.

Her cotton receipts reached five hundred thousand bales last year — an increase of sixty thousand over the year before. Out from her healthy commercial heart issue five trunk lines of railway; and a sixth is being added.

—*Life on the Mississippi*, 1883, Chapter 29

A couple blocks from my hotel was the Cotton Exchange Museum, housed in a 1939 building that John Grisham used as a setting for his 1991 novel The Firm. The museum's displays bring back to life the days when cotton was king, when Memphis's warehouses bulged with bales of cotton brought by steamboats from plantations all along the Mississippi, when the mournful music of the slaves who picked the cotton gave birth to the blues.

A good place to examine a city's history is in an old cemetery. So I contacted representatives of Volunteer Mid-South and accompanied them on a visit to another of the organization's projects: the Zion Christian Cemetery.

Established in 1876 by the United Sons of Zion, a black fraternal and benevolent organization made up of former slaves, the cemetery is the oldest African-American burial place in Memphis. The graveyard was used until the 1970s.

But not long after its last burial, it became an abandoned, neglected tract overgrown with kudzu and weeds. In the 1980s and 1990s, the old graveyard was a clandestine chop shop for car thieves and a dumping ground for trash ranging from old tires to disposable diapers.

Cutting through the underbrush with machetes, local activist Ken Hall and I explored the center of the 15-acre property, where, in the shade of an ancient magnolia tree, we uncovered a long-forgotten treasure.

"This obelisk represents the family of Dr. Georgia Patton Washington, the first female African-American physician in the state," Ken said.

The obelisk had toppled from it base and lay half-covered by kudzu. Ken swept away the vegetation to reveal the inscription: "DR. G.E.L. PATTON - WIFE OF DAVID W. WASHINGTON - BORN APRIL 16, 1864 - DIED NOV 8, 1900."

As it lay, the marble and limestone obelisk was 10 feet long and bore on its sides the names of family members, including a boy named Willie who died the same day he was born, in the year before the passing of Dr. Washington.

I knew a bit about the history of the cemetery, but I asked Ken for an overview.

"The idea was to have here – which at that time was on the outskirts of Memphis – a final resting place of dignity for African-Americans," he said.

But because the cemetery was the project of a relatively small group of people, the United Sons of Zion, and not connected with a church or institution, "it began to decline precipitously" as its founders and their immediate family began to age and die off.

"So we see, by the 1920s and 1930s, some notations from health departments and other agencies citing this cemetery for hazards and problems," Ken said. "Another difficulty is that the first 20 years – from 1876 to 1896 – the records of burials were lost. We currently have records from between 1896 to about 1968. There were very few burials after the 1950s. We know of at least 22,000 people buried here but it could be a few thousand more."

I asked Ken what other notable African-Americans might be buried here. He said that some of the graves of historical figures, like that of Dr. Washington, have been found and identified but that others have yet to be discovered and cleared.

"There is an infant daughter of W.C. Handy, father of the blues," he said. "Some lynching victims from the 1890s – a very significant, turbulent time here. I'm told that the grandparents of Benjamin Hooks, the former national director of the NAACP are in here somewhere. It's just a matter of uncovering the existing overgrowth to find these headstones."

Gesturing at the acres of rampant foliage – weeds, kudzu and thorn bushes, Ken said: "And they're somewhere under this."

I will gradually drop this subject of graveyards. I have been trying all I could to get down to the sentimental part of it, but I cannot accomplish it. I think there is no genuinely sentimental part to it. It is all grotesque, ghastly, horrible.

—*Life on the Mississippi,* 1883, Chapter 42

Ken spoke admiringly of the volunteers who have worked on the Zion Community Project, from colleges, churches, businesses and youth groups – including about a hundred local teens from the nonprofit Bridge Builders, who came out with machetes, mowers and clippers to help reclaim the land.

"I think whether you have faith-based folks, or people that are simply concerned about history, the idea that there is something to bring people together on this project, from all walks of life, speaks about the innate goodness in people and their desire to do right," Ken said. "This is 22,000-plus final resting places that deserve some respect and dignity – and that resonates with a lot of people."

Memphis is striving to make the city, in life and in death, a "place of good abode."

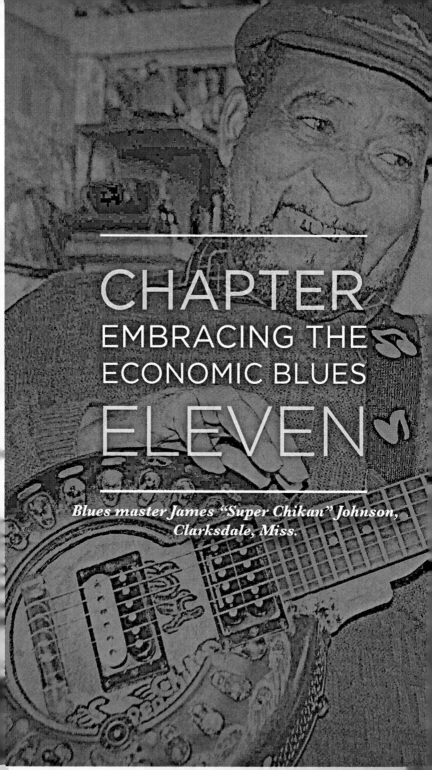

CHAPTER
EMBRACING THE
ECONOMIC BLUES
ELEVEN

*Blues master James "Super Chikan" Johnson,
Clarksdale, Miss.*

I N THE PARLANCE OF THE BLUES, a common
means of transport for someone down and out and
alone in the world might be a southbound train, a beat-
up pickup, maybe an old Chevy. I don't recall any blues song
that mentions a canoe.

I wasn't quite down and out, but I certainly felt alone as
I paddled my canoe down the sinuous course of the Mississippi
River from Memphis. A pack of wild dogs on the Arkansas
side, where I had camped, kept me awake with their howling
the night before, magnifying my lonesome feeling.

And yet I was filled with giddy excitement as I paddled past the state line between Tennessee and Mississippi and neared the heart and soul of the Mississippi Delta, the self-proclaimed cradle of the blues. I've long been a devotee of the blues, and here in the Mississippi Delta I hoped to meet some of the genre's living legends.

The Mississippi Delta shouldn't be confused with the Mississippi River Delta, about 300 miles to the south where the Mississippi empties into the Gulf of Mexico. The Mississippi Delta is a vast, table-flat alluvial plain in the shape of an almond between the Mississippi and Yazoo rivers in northwestern Mississippi. Centuries of flooding between the two rivers have deposited some of the richest soil on the planet. Cotton was king here, and the African-Americans who worked the plantations were the progenitors of the blues.

I was met at the river and driven to Clarksdale by John Ruskey, an intense, middle-aged man with unkempt wisps of hair who had rafted the Mississippi in 1982. A Colorado native and first curator of the Delta Blues Museum in Clarksdale, Ruskey is also a canoe builder and founder of the Quapaw Canoe Co., which runs canoe and kayak trips out of Clarksdale and Helena, on the Arkansas side where I had put in.

The Mississippi River has changed course many times over the years and once flowed past downtown Clarksdale. The river is now about 10 miles to the west. As we headed for Clarksdale in Ruskey's 4-by-4 along U.S. 61, I figured he was sizing me up, trying to determine whether I had the right stuff to make it to New Orleans. But I was wrong. His mind was on something else.

As we neared Clarksdale at sunset, he pulled his truck off the highway onto a patch of land that looked like it might once have been part of a cotton plantation. He directed me to a particular spot on the land and we stared at it in silence.

Behind other islands we found wretched little farms, and wretcheder little log-cabins; there were crazy rail fences sticking a foot or two above the water, with one or two jeans-clad, chills-racked, yellow-faced male miserables roosting on the top rail, elbows on knees, jaws in hands, grinding tobacco and discharging the result at floating chips through crevices left by lost teeth; while the rest of the family and the few farm-animals were huddled together in an empty wood-flat riding at her moorings close at hand. In this flat-boat the family would have to cook and eat and sleep for a lesser or greater number of days (or possibly weeks), until the river should fall two or three feet and let them get back to their log-cabin and their chills again – chills being a merciful provision of an all-wise Providence to enable them to take exercise without exertion. And this sort of watery camping out was a thing which these people were rather liable to be treated to a couple of times a year: by the December rise out of the Ohio, and the June rise out of the Mississippi. And yet these were kindly dispensations, for they at least enabled the poor things to rise from the dead now and then, and look upon life when a steamboat went by. They appreciated the blessing,

too, for they spread their mouths and eyes wide open and made the
most of these occasions. Now what could these banished creatures find
to do to keep from dying of the blues during the low-water season!

—*Life on the Mississippi*, 1883, Chapter 11

"This was Muddy Waters' place," Ruskey said in a tone of reverence, breaking the silence.

Born as McKinley Morganfield in Jug's Corner, Miss., in 1913, the blues musician who became known as Muddy Waters had lived here as a boy in a cabin made of cypress planks. The reconstructed cabin is now on display at the Delta Blues Museum where Ruskey was curator.

I knew a little bit about how American roots music evolved in the Mississippi Delta – how slaves brought their stories and music from Africa, how their plantation work songs and spirituals led to the blues and how Mississippi Delta bluesmen like Robert Johnson and Muddy Waters influenced such rock 'n' roll musicians as Mick Jagger and Keith Richards of the Rolling Stones and Robert Plant of Led Zeppelin.

And here I was in the place that calls itself "the birthplace of the blues." I was so excited that I was shaking in my Muck Boots.

John – friendships on the river quickly progress to a first-name basis – allowed me to take up residence in his canoe shop. I pitched my tent inside to keep the mosquitos from dining on me, and at first light I stepped out into the streets of Clarksdale to take a look around. As I walked around the town, I heard the voice of Robert Johnson, called the "king of the Delta blues singers," coming from shop windows and passing cars. The intersection of U.S. 61 and U.S. 69 at Clarksdale is said to be the crossroads where Johnson sold his soul to the devil in exchange for his guitar virtuosity. Some say that the local version of that Faustian legend comes from a report that Johnson dropped out of sight for a time in the early 1930s and returned as a much better guitar player.

Whether or not folks in Clarksdale believe the story, there certainly is respect here for those first-generation bluesmen, whose music is enjoying a revival. During my walk, I struck up a conversion with an elderly black man on a bench outside a local eatery. He wore a felt hat and a black-silk Aloha shirt and was rolling a pair of dice back and forth in his hands. He invited me to sit with him a spell.

"My name is Obbie Lee Barnes, but they all call me Puttin' Hatchet," he said, rolling a toothpick from side to side on his lower lip. "I've been here in this town since 1937."

When talk turned to the blues, Puttin' Hatchet seemed to be the go-to guy on the subject. "I know the son of Bob Williams," he said. "I know Riley B. King. I know Super Chikan. I know Bobby Moore. I know *all* the blues singers."

Puttin' Hatchett, 80, said he made a living playing cards and rolling dice. He let me snap his photo on the sidewalk and again inside the café, where he posed next to a framed black-and-white photograph of his younger self – complete with hat and toothpick, but with the nine of clubs, instead of dice, in his hand.

The sun was at its zenith when I left the café and walked a block or so down Delta Avenue to a shop called Cat Head Delta Blues & Folk Art. The young man behind the counter, sporting a beard and shaved head, introduced himself as Sean "Bad" Apple and said he was a musician. I was struck by his nickname, "Bad," because he was very friendly and seemed to come from a middle-class background. He said he had come to this mecca of the blues to learn the genre firsthand from an early-generation bluesman who'd take the time to teach him on his porch – and that he was enjoying Clarksdale more than any place he'd ever lived.

He asked what I was doing in town and I told him that I hoped to interview Super Chikan, whose real name is James Johnson, as a "citizen journalist" for CNN. He laughed heartily and suggested that I drop the "citizen" part of my introduction if I met Super Chikan. Bad Apple seemed to doubt my bona fides until I produced Super Chikan's home phone number, given to me by the Blues Foundation in Memphis. "OK, let me do you a favor," he said. "I'll go ahead and call on your behalf." Bad Apple picked up the phone and, after some pleasantries, said: "We've got a hack, a right proper fool, here who says he's a 'citizen journalist,' whatever the hell that means, for CNN, and wants to interview you." He laughed and added: "But in all actuality he looks harmless enough."

I had told Bad Apple that I'd be in town for a week. After hanging up, he said there was no way that I'd get an interview with Super Chikan, just like that, but that if I were lucky he might just fit me in on my final day in Clarksdale.

Bad Apple was on the phone again, this time with a tourist asking directions. So I looked around the shop, filled with a blend of CDs by local musicians and others beyond Clarksdale, called "outsider art." I found an imported CD called *Chikadelic* for $20. Super Chikan had recorded it in Norway and the label said: "Not Available in the U.S."

As I browsed, one of the local talents whose work was featured in the store pulled up on a beat-up cruiser bike toting a guitar case. He was Foster Wiley, known as "Mr. Tater the Music Maker," said to be the last surviving street performer in the Mississippi Delta. The executive director of the Delta Blues Museum would later describe "Mr. Tater" to me as "the hardest working man in show business – who is not in show business."

In front of the Cat Head, Mr. Tater plugged in his battered Crate amp, strummed a few times on his red Squier Stratocaster and plunged into a routine he'd probably performed hundreds of times in Clarksdale. He agreed to an interview so we sat together to talk on an old church pew in front of the Cat Head.

"How does it feel when you play the blues?" I asked.

"Ah, it make me feel good," Mr. Tater said with one of the sweetest smiles I'd ever seen. "It make me feel happy."

Mr. Tater, who looked to be in his early 60s, had a pair of gray sideburns sticking out from his blue knit cap. He lived and breathed the blues, usually playing by day at the Cat Head. He'd then hop on his bike, equipped at the front with a big wire basket to haul his gear, to make his nighttime rounds of the local juke joints. If he were lucky, he'd maybe get a chance to jam inside once the headlined band stepped down.

He handed me a flyer for Club 2000, where he hoped he'd be playing later that week. And then he was gone, off to play his next sidewalk gig.

Little did we know, as we sat talking on that early fall day, that Mr. Tater would die of kidney failure about a year later, on Sept. 10, 2010, in the intensive care unit at Methodist University Hospital in Memphis. He was believed to be 63.

I hung out at the Cat Head for the rest of the day and met the employee who relieved Bad Apple. LaLa Craig, also a musician, wore a red beret bedecked with souvenir pins promoting concerts or musicians. She surveyed the shop with her elbow resting on the counter and her hand cupping her chin, putting on a broad smile for the customers and this canoeing journalist who wanted to learn more about the blues. It was apparent that the Cat Head was information central for the local music scene.

I also met Roger Stolle, owner and founder of the Cat Head. He has traveled the region to befriend and interview the last of the first generation of bluesmen for a series of film documentaries. He spoke of the optimism and resilience of the early blues musicians, despite the troubles they'd experienced, and said these traits are often reflected in their music.

He cited as an example James Lewis Carter Ford, an old bluesman who goes by the name T-Model Ford and often includes in his act a song called "Nobody Gets Me Down."

"He'll talk about being hit in the head with a chair, getting stabbed, you know, whatever's happening in life – and nothing gets him down, he keeps on going," Roger said.

"There's a guy named CeDell Davis, who lives on the other side of the river, over in Arkansas, and very much the same thing – he went through polio, got trampled in a juke joint. He used to play guitar, and now he's had a stroke and can't play guitar but he still sings. And these are guys that nothing will keep them down.

"Whether you're dealing with trying to make money and live or just waking up every morning with a smile – these are guys who are able to do it," Roger continued. "And I think the music and sort of the history behind it helps them do it."

On Bad Apple's recommendation, I went that night to Tricia's Italian Restaurant and Pie Hole to catch a performance of an up-and-coming blues singer named Mary Ann "Action" Jackson. Bad Apple said he'd be playing in the band that night and that I most certainly shouldn't miss her act.

To get to the pizza joint, off the main thoroughfare, Delta Avenue, I walked under a blanket of stars through a maze of alleys. At the door, I paid a $5 cover charge that included a first drink. When I arrived, more people were on stage setting up than in the audience and I wondered if I'd be the only paying customer. I took a seat with my complimentary Coors Light.

But by the time Action Jackson took to the makeshift stage and grabbed the mic, the seats had filled and the place had been transformed from pizza parlor to juke joint. "We're the All Night Long Blues Band," she announced to raucous cheers and whistles. Bad Apple was on lead guitar and female musicians played bass and shook the tambourines. A huge white guy, who looked like he had walked out of the film *O Brother, Where Art Thou?*, strutted about the stage, huffing and puffing on a harmonica. Wearing a gold hat and dress and a necklace of crocodile teeth, Action Jackson lived up to her name. Her exuberance was infectious as she cavorted on the stage, interacting with the audience. The joint was jumping and jiving. It was a fairly typical night in Clarksdale – a town where the blues is a religion and Tricia's Italian Restaurant and Pie Hole is a church.

"Blues was the music that people listened to help escape their troubles," Jay Sieleman, executive director of the Blues Foundation, had told me upriver in Memphis. "Blues music is what people do to get rid of the blues. They went out on a Saturday afternoon or Saturday night and celebrated – and they did it through blues music. So blues music doesn't give you the blues – it helps take away your blues. That's the significance. And I think that's why it's as popular today as it's ever been. And also why it'll be around forever."

We have all had the "blues" – the mere sky-blues – but mine were indigo...
—*Roughing It, 1872,* Chapter 40

Between sets, Action Jackson took a breather out front on the sidewalk and I had a chance to find out more about her. She's a mother of three and grandmother of eight. She said she drives down from Memphis – "60 miles, every weekend" – to perform in Clarksdale, "because it's an inspiration."

I asked about the role of the blues in this time of economic hardship. "The blues will make you feel better," Mary said, her earrings catching the glow of the neon Bud Light sign in the window. "If you can get your mind on the blues, you will not even think about the economics – because it's an inside thing. It's a soul feeling – it comes from the inside out, not from the outside in, and when you think about the inside, you won't even think about the economics of the world. You forget about the cares of the world, you know, and just hum in your spirit and in your soul."

Within two minutes, or even less, he had forgotten all his troubles. Not because his troubles were one whit less heavy and bitter to him than a man's are to a man, but because a new and powerful interest bore them down and drove them out of his mind for the time — just as men's misfortunes are forgotten in the excitement of new enterprises. This new interest was a valued novelty in whistling, which he had just acquired from a negro, and he was suffering to practice it undisturbed. It consisted in a peculiar bird-like turn, a sort of liquid warble, produced by touching the tongue to the roof of the mouth at short intervals in the midst of the music — the reader probably remembers how to do it, if he has ever been a boy. Diligence and attention soon gave him the knack of it, and he strode down the street with his mouth full of harmony and his soul full of gratitude. He felt much as an astronomer feels who has discovered a new planet — no doubt, as far as strong, deep, unalloyed pleasure is concerned, the advantage was with the boy, not the astronomer.

—*The Adventures of Tom Sawyer,* 1876, Chapter 1

"Economics, that word just keep gettin' in the way," Mary went on. "I try not to even think about the economics, man, 'cause like I say, it's stressful. Economics is stressful. I just take one day at a time and like I said, I really don't worry about it. I'm just a Mississippi woman — I've got Mississippi mud on my shoes."

As I walked back to my lodgings that night, nursing a half-finished bottle of Southern Comfort, Mary's music echoed in my brain. I thought of the words of Jay Sieleman, who had spoken to me in Memphis in front of a wall full of framed photos of black blues legends. "That's the historical significance," he had said of the blues. "It came from the least of the least and yet it spread out all over the world to become this very important music, not only in itself, but also in its impact on other types of music – jazz, rock 'n' roll, hip hop, soul, R&B – you name it."

I awoke early the next morning for a walk around Clarksdale, but soon realized that it was Sunday and that everything was closed. Back at the Quapaw Canoe Co., my stomach grumbling for food, I saw John out front, loading a huge, custom-built, cedar-strip canoe onto a trailer for a weekend outing. I asked where I might find some company and something to eat.

"You follow this street down, across the tracks, just past Red's juke joint," he said. "Make a left and you'll find a row of churches, about a mile down, all lined up. Look for the steeple, enter a church, and there you'll find all the people."

I rustled up a clean shirt, washed my face and combed my hair and headed out for Sunday worship. The churches were indeed lined up, just past the town cemetery. As I approached the first one, an edifice of red brick with white columns and a pretty steeple, an elderly lady at the front door beckoned me in. "Come and partake, child," she beamed. "The service has done started, but you're welcome."

The sign out front read: "Haven United Methodist Church, Worship Service 11:00 AM, PASTOR Rev. Ozell

Landfair." The church was packed, and I quickly noticed that I was the only white. I stood awkwardly at the back until a family squeezed together and made space in the last row. An elderly gentleman in the pew, who wore a tweed jacket and bowtie, wrapped an arm around my shoulder and slapped me on the back as I sat down.

In his homily, Pastor Landfair told a story about a boy on a train who didn't have a ticket. The conductor put him off and none of the paying passengers objected, the pastor said, until the train broke down not far from the station. An old woman, seeing the hand of Providence, stood up and told the conductor that he shouldn't have left the boy. His voice rising as he neared the end of the homily, the pastor soundly rebuked those who see wrong and do nothing. "For it was because they'd abandoned him, the train had come to a stop," he said. Bringing the story's message closer to home, he added: "We have a lot of young males in jail and we need to pray for them."

The pastor looked toward a group of teenaged boys sitting together in a side row. "Don't be too proud to change your circumstance, too proud to change your condition," he said. "There's a bright side somewhere. Don't you stop 'til you find it … Keep rolling on." Then the choir stood, its members swaying from side to side in time with the hymn, and sang out words that reinforced the pastor's message: "Deep in your heart, deep in your soul, keep holding on. There's a bright side somewhere."

On the steps of the church after the service, Pastor Landfair spoke to me about the tenacity and resilience of his congregation, and of the people in Clarksdale generally.

"I want to say we can survive regardless of what befalls us," he said, standing in the sunshine of a glorious day. "We can survive. And we find ways and means to survive. This area, when you look at rural Mississippi, Clarksdale as a whole has a rich history as it relates to the blues. And the whole country, not just this country, but the world, can learn from Clarksdale."

The pastor was called away by his family, and the man in the bow tie joined me. Today was someone's birthday and, before I could decline, I was ushered downstairs where members of the congregation milled about in a hall filled with tables and chairs. A space was made for me at one of the tables, and before I quite realized what was going on, I was handed a paper plate, utensils and a cold Coca-Cola. Large ladies behind long tables laden with comfort food were dishing out piles of spareribs, grits, succotash and other home-cooked delicacies.

My plate piled high, I stood there in happy reverie, recalling a time during my childhood in Los Angeles. On Sundays when I was about 9, my mother would take me along on visits to a dear friend, an elderly black woman whom I knew as Mrs. Washington. Going to her home was like stepping into a different world. Its walls were hung with photographs from an earlier time, in a different city. Mrs. Washington was nearly blind, and, as she lovingly fondled these images of her past life, I sat on her crochet-covered couch and listened intently to the most enthralling stories I had ever heard.

When Mrs. Washington fell sick and lay near death in the intensive care unit of a local hospital, she had no family to visit her. My mother went to the hospital, but a nurse told her that only immediate family would be allowed at Mrs. Washington's bedside. "Well that's just fine," my spunky mother said, "for this woman is my sister." The nurse obviously knew that this white woman wasn't really Mrs. Washington's sister, but she allowed her to sit at the bedside to hold the hand of her old friend and to say goodbye. I cried when Mrs. Washington died, and it wasn't until years later – after my mother had also passed – that I learned how the two had become friends. Mrs. Washington and my mother had lived in the same Los Angeles neighborhood when my mom was a girl. In the 1930s and 1940s, the neighborhood was home to many Scottish immigrants. It's now called South-Central LA.

————

The story of the blues is as transient as the water of the Mississippi River. And, indeed, it was the river that helped spread this uniquely American genre of music – upriver to towns like Memphis and St. Louis, and then on to Chicago and Kansas City and the world.

"The blues come from down south," Action Jackson had told me the night before. "And, as you know, everything that came from down south went up north. But they done come back from up north to down south … down south where we can just breathe in good fresh air."

But some who sing the blues have never felt the need to migrate north, or move out of Clarksdale, for that matter. One of them is Super Chikan, the intended subject of an interview even before I had set foot in the town.

On the last day of my stay in Clarksdale, news came that Super Chikan was ready to talk to me. "He feels bad," said my host John Ruskey, a friend of the local legend. "He wanted to make time for you that first day but he had a funeral to attend and sing at and he wanted to focus on that. So he's said he's gonna give you all the time you want today."

John drove me to Super Chikan's house where he met us on the front lawn, paintbrush in hand working on a piece of artwork. Super Chikan is a man of many talents – blues musician, artist and maker of guitars. John introduced me, said I was an OK guy and offered to pick me up later. But Super Chikan said that, no, he'd drive me back to the canoe shop when we were finished.

James "Super Chikan" Johnson said that the workshop behind his house, which he calls the "chicken shack," is a work in progress. He's expanding it to make more room to work on his art and guitars. He showed me a wide variety of the homemade instruments that he plays and sells. There was a didleybo hybrid that he calls a "bojo," his LeghornRooster guitar, an ax guitar, .38 caliber gun guitar, and some whose bodies were made from the motor housings of ceiling fans. They're not just musical instruments, but works of folk art, elaborately painted and studded with decorative geegaws. A simple cigar box guitar will set you back around $3,800, while a diddleybo bojo will run close to $5,000. And they sell.

Super Chikan took a seat in the middle of his shop as I set up my cameras, using a row of his guitars as a backdrop. He suddenly got up, hurried to the house and came back wearing a flat wool cap decorated with images of – you guessed it – chickens. He asked how he looked. I said, "Mighty fine," pressed "record," and asked how he got into the blues.

"It was never a plan to be a musician," he said, as smoke from a cigarette wreathed his face. "There were always instruments and musicians around the house. I just played because everybody else played."

He said blues was what everybody liked and wanted to hear. "People like Jimmy Reed, Muddy Waters, Johnny Lee Hooker, Willie Dickson, Slim Harpo – people like that used to come around my grandpa's and play a lot," he said. "My grandpa was a fiddler. His name was Ellis Johnson, and he was a musician and a Mason as well. Well, most of the old musicians was secret Masons – they worked the Underground Railroad. And they would have their meetings at my grandpa's house and he would call it a front porch party and they would all play and have a good time and have their meeting and then get about their business. And so I wound up being a musician not trying to.

"Well, you may hear some Jimmy Reed in me 'cause Jimmy Reed was one of my mentors," Super Chikan continued. "And I liked him 'cause he would always crack jokes about us. He called us 'crumb snatchers.'"

He said Reed would gesture toward the children and ask his grandfather: "Brother Johnson, how you feed all them crumb snatchers out there?" Then he'd add: "You give 'em a drink of this moonshine and they quit eatin'."

Super Chikan had to laugh at the memory. "He would jive with us, you know, carry on with us," he said. "Back in the day, young men had respect for older people – kids had respect. A kid would be afraid to walk through a crowd of old people. Today, it's just the opposite. Older people are afraid to walk through a crowd of kids."

Back to how he got into the music business, he said: "As I got older, when it came down to jobs and everything, I said, what else do I know how to do? ... And so I said, shoot, I can play music, but my intention was just to write songs.

"During my truck drivin' years, I heard on the radio that songwriters was makin' more money than the entertainers, the performers. So I said, man, I can write a song, so that was my intention – to just write songs for all the other musicians.

But Jim O'Neal, who had Rooster Records, he enticed me to do the singin' myself. He said, 'These songs are all you. It's got a meaning, it's got a feeling, and it would be just words to somebody else, but it would be you if you sang them yourself. 'Cause you know what you were about, what you were thinking and how you felt.' So we went from there."

Super Chikan played four or five songs for me that afternoon in his workshop, including "Front Porch Boogie" and "Sittin' on the Pecan Tree." Toward the end of the interview I asked about the importance of passing the traditions and musicianship of the blues from one generation to the next.

"What you do is hope, because you know as each generation come around, everything changes and everybody changes and their way of life changes so you're hoping that there's somebody in that generation or in that family will pick up what you're doing and take after you and do what you're doin'," he said. "I was one that did it. It didn't seem like it meant much at the time, but now, today, it's paying off for me. It got to be a valuable trade. And so I'm hopin' that somebody in this generation will pick up what I'm doin' and carry it on because the link to the past is dyin' out.

"I'm one of the links to the past and so I'm hanging in there with it," he said. "Today, according to the people and fans, I'm famous … But me, until I've got something to match that fame, I don't think I'm famous yet. Until I live like a famous man – and then I'm famous."

We talked about Clarksdale's claim that it's the birthplace of the blues. Super Chikan observed that the slogan, used by the city on its website and by local boosters to attract tourists, goes much deeper than the music – that's it's more about the hard lives that produced the music.

"That's why most of the guys left," he said, referring to the migration of African-Americans to northern cities. "They were so glad to get out of the field. They didn't want to be nowhere near it, they didn't want to be a part of it, so they took off up north and, as a matter of fact, a whole bunch of them disowned Mississippi."

But Super Chikan said he decided to stay here "to find out how far a poor boy could go bein' himself." He said he has lived in Clarksdale all his life, "and I learned how to live with the people here, without frowning every day."

We were getting down now into the migrating negro region. These poor people could never travel when they were slaves; so they make up for the privation now. They stay on a plantation till the desire to travel seizes them; then they pack up, hail a steamboat, and clear out. Not for any particular place; no, nearly any place will answer; they only want to be moving. The amount of money on hand will answer the rest of the conundrum for them. If it will take them fifty miles, very well; let it be fifty. If not, a shorter flight will do.

—*Life on the Mississippi*, 1883, Chapter 30

From preaching, to laughing, to playing, to reflecting, Super Chikan wrapped up our time together with a simple statement that captured the mood of a nation in hard times.

"There's a lot of us in a strain right now," he said. "A lot of us got the blues and don't even play it. And don't sing it. But we cry it every day."

The next day, I boarded a Delta Lines bus to begin a roundabout journey that would take me to the university town of Oxford, Miss. Oxford, I reckoned, would be a good place to provide a respite from the river and to get a start on this book. But I was reluctant to leave Clarksdale, and memories of the remarkable people I met here kept coming back to me. As the bus rolled out of the small terminal on North State Street, I recalled the words of Obbie Lee "Puttin' Hatchett" Barnes as we sat on that bench outside a Clarksdale eatery:

"People come here from everywhere to hear the blues. They be at Red's tonight to hear the blues, they be at different places to hear the blues. The blues is everywhere you go. You play somethin' else, you ain't gonna make your money. You're gonna make your money when you start playin' the blues."

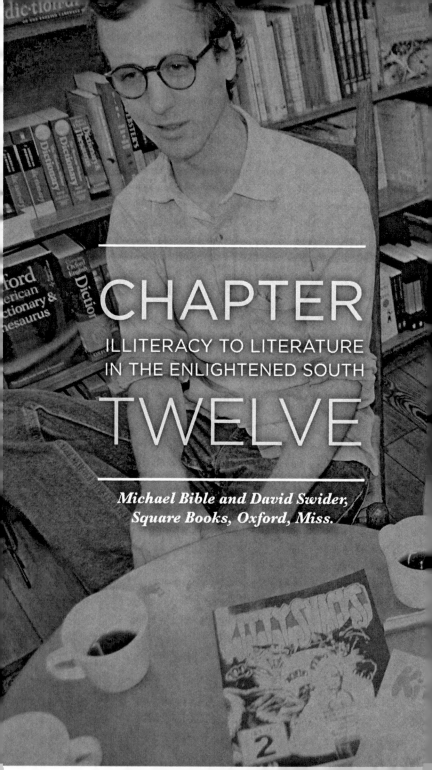

CHAPTER

ILLITERACY TO LITERATURE
IN THE ENLIGHTENED SOUTH

TWELVE

*Michael Bible and David Swider,
Square Books, Oxford, Miss.*

THE STEADY THRUM OF tires on a highway was a sound I was becoming reacquainted with after weeks on the river listening to the water rippling beneath my canoe. My bus was rolling north up U.S. 61, flat and straight on the alluvial plane. I was headed for Memphis, the first stop of a circuitous journey that would bring me south again to Tupelo, Miss., in quest of a story that didn't pan out, and then on to Oxford.

In Oxford, I planned to take a rest from the Mississippi River, to assemble the stories I had collected so far and to see if I might have the makings of a book. What better place to do it, I thought, than Oxford. It's the home of the University of Mississippi, or Ole Miss, a repository of knowledge on the history and lore of the South. It's where William Faulkner, one of the South's preeminent writers, lived and worked in a colonnaded Greek Revival mansion called Rowan Oak. It has Thacker Mountain Radio, a live radio show featuring an eclectic mix of music and stories broadcast weekly from Oxford's town square. And, also on the Square, is a wonderful bookstore called Square Books, a place where a good writer is like a rock star, where literature is parsed and critiqued over endless cups of coffee. I was no Faulkner, I figured, but maybe the muse will strike me there.

A low-budget motel that I checked into upon arriving in Oxford had touted itself as being "a stone's throw from the Oxford Square." But it turned out to be in a nondescript area of strip shopping centers and chain restaurants. After a night of restless sleep in a place that seemed like it was miles from the literary ambience I was seeking in Oxford, I dispatched a distress call to one of my friends in Hannibal, Cindy Lovell of the Mark Twain Boyhood Home & Museum. She promptly telephoned the University of Mississippi Museum, which looks after Rowan Oak, to ask for a lead on a back yard closer to town where I might pitch my tent.

A short time later, Bob Pekala, the museum preparator

who took Cindy's call, rolled up at my motel in his Ford King Ranch pickup and yelled from the truck, "Come on, hop up and hop in!" He had asked on the phone if I had a tie, on account of where we were headed for lunch. When I told him no, he said, "Not to worry. I'm not going to wear one either. We'll be fine." Our quick tour of Oxford took us to a grand circular drive at the end of a cul-de-sac. "That's where you'll be staying," he said, "out back in the guest quarters – two bedrooms, a lounge, and bathroom. You'll have a direct view out onto Rowan Oak, through the trees this time of year, and direct use of the swimming pool, which you'll be expected to help me keep clean." This place, I realized, was Bob's home. "Oh," he added, "meals will be made available courtesy of my lovely wife, Jane."

I had heard all about Southern hospitality, of course, but this was over the top. What a grand place to take a vacation from the river! I'd be lodging next to the home of one of America's greatest authors on a picturesque street lined with 19th-century wooden houses and lorded over by majestic cedar and oak trees. And I'd be within a short walk of the Square.

"You understand, I needed to meet you first-hand before I introduced you to my wife," Bob explained, looking me squarely in the eyes. "We're lucky enough to have one of the nicest parcels of real estate in town, four acres in total, directly bordering Rowan Oak. And we like nothing more than to share it with friends. I hope it will do."

Will it do? I couldn't believe my luck.

Because I lacked a tie, Bob had suggested that I wear a nice shirt. That would make me sufficiently presentable for the weekly luncheon of Oxford's Rotarians at the University Club, just off the Square. It was a members-only establishment with cherry wood-paneled walls, a grand piano, subdued lighting, antique crystal, bone china and a covey of servers with white cloths draped over their arms.

As Bob introduced me around our table, I was taken aback when a young lawyer named Brad Mayo said to me: "I know you. You're that roving reporter. I caught your interview out front of Ground Zero with Bill Luckett … I came home from work and had four emails, all from different friends, telling me, 'You've gotta check this out.'"

He was referring to an interview I had done with Luckett outside a Clarksdale blues club called Ground Zero. Luckett, a lawyer and business partner of actor Morgan Freeman, was making a long-shot run for Mississippi governor.

The others at the table nodded in my direction, as if putting into context this rumpled interloper. A look around the room would tell even an outsider that this was a gathering place for those of a certain pedigree and profession, a Who's Who of Oxford. The young lawyer at our table probably considered himself fortunate to be there; his star was obviously on the rise.

My only connection to these pillars of the town was Bob,

who sat back in his chair seemingly indifferent to the formality of the occasion. I was beginning to feel more comfortable when the presiding Rotarian tapped a crystal decanter with his spoon and called for silence. I cringed when it came time for the introduction of guests. One well-groomed gent after another rose at a table and announced to the august gathering something along these lines: I'd like to introduce so and so, ex-Airborne, Ole Miss law, a leader in his profession for 25 years, etc., etc. Each person being introduced seemed more illustrious than the one before and was welcomed by a round of applause and a chorus of "Here, here!"

Then came time for my introduction. Bob stood up, cleared his throat, put an arm around my shoulder and declared: "This is Neal Moore, a free-lance journalist with CNN who is floating down the Mississippi on a canoe." The introduction was followed by dead silence, none of the audience seeming to know how to respond. After an awkward lull, the master of ceremonies remarked, "You're heading down to New Orleans, I presume?" "Yes," I said, shifting back and forth on my feet. "The French Quarter." To which he delivered a deadpan reply: "I hope you make it." And the audience finally found reason to applaud.

> *From Cairo to Baton Rouge, when the river is over its banks, you have no particular trouble in the night, for the thousand-mile wall of dense forest that guards the two banks all the way is only gapped with a farm or wood-yard opening at intervals, and so you can't 'get*

out of the river' much easier than you could get out of a fenced lane; but from Baton Rouge to New Orleans it is a different matter. The river is more than a mile wide, and very deep – as much as two hundred feet, in places. Both banks, for a good deal over a hundred miles, are shorn of their timber and bordered by continuous sugar plantations, with only here and there a scattering sapling or row of ornamental China-trees. The timber is shorn off clear to the rear of the plantations, from two to four miles. When the first frost threatens to come, the planters snatch off their crops in a hurry. When they have finished grinding the cane, they form the refuse of the stalks (which they call BAGASSE) into great piles and set fire to them, though in other sugar countries the bagasse is used for fuel in the furnaces of the sugar mills. Now the piles of damp bagasse burn slowly, and smoke like Satan's own kitchen.

An embankment ten or fifteen feet high guards both banks of the Mississippi all the way down that lower end of the river, and this embankment is set back from the edge of the shore from ten to perhaps a hundred feet, according to circumstances; say thirty or forty feet, as a general thing. Fill that whole region with an impenetrable gloom of smoke from a hundred miles of burning bagasse piles, when the river is over the banks, and turn a steamboat loose along there at midnight and see how she will feel. And see how you will feel, too! You find yourself away out in the midst of a vague dim sea that is shoreless, that fades out and loses itself in the murky distances; for you cannot discern the thin rib of embankment, and you are always imagining you see a straggling tree when you don't.

—*Life on the Mississippi,* 1883, Chapter 11

Baptism by fire, I thought. "I wanted to see how you'd stand up, how you'd do with a crowd like this – and you did just fine," Bob whispered into my ear. Now it was my turn to clap him on the back.

As we tucked into our lunch, the featured speaker took the podium. She was Dr. Jo Ann O'Quin of the University of Mississippi's Department of Social Work. She spoke from the heart about her 25-year career in Alzheimer's research, urged the audience to take part in Oxford's first annual Memory Walk coming up that weekend and asked for a show of hands of those who had a relative or friend stricken by the debilitating brain disease. Nearly everyone raised a hand. "The sign-up sheet is making the rounds," she said. "We need you to sign up to support a walking team. Yes, we need your help, financially, but more important than that, we need you to take a stand."

I had never known anyone with Alzheimer's, but the passion in Dr. O'Quin's speech prompted me to approach her after the benediction. "I was touched by your presentation," I said, "and although I'm here to do a different story, I'd like to cover yours as well." She smiled and suggested Beth and Jay VanWinkle as likely interview subjects.

I awoke the next morning to the chirping of blue jays

and a view from the window of a family of deer grazing on a manicured lawn that stretched to the woods. Propped against the pillows of my antique brass bedstead, I could also see Rowan Oak, nestled amid pine, sweetgum and oak trees. There was a rap at the door announcing breakfast, and after a quick shower I was ushered into the main house to dine with the Pekalas.

Jane Pekala, originally from the Delta, was a charming, delightful woman with a motherly smile. She and Bob had met in Oxford and they had been married for three years. Bob, I learned, was originally from Pittsfield, Mass., but his work and studies had taken him to such places as New York, Britain, Greece, Israel and India. Before coming to Oxford, he had worked in Cambridge, Mass., for the Harvard University Art Museums – the Fogg, the Busch-Reisinger and the Sackler.

We were all running in different directions that morning, but we promised to regroup for dinner in the evening. I walked out to the street armed with a map of Oxford, a notebook and a brace of cameras. A cool breeze rustled through the Southern red oaks and hazelnut trees, their autumn foliage a riot of red and gold, as I headed toward the Square.

A stroll through Oxford, with its antique grandeur and air of bygone gentility, is a bit like entering a time warp. I followed the example of the older gentlemen of the town and tipped my hat to passing ladies. Some townsfolk stopped to shake my hand and chat. Thanks to a story in the *Oxford Eagle*, they were familiar with my face and name.

In and near the Square are such convivial establishments as the Ajax Diner, the Bottletree Bakery and the Blind Pig Pub and Deli. Situated directly across the Square from the courthouse, where the Square meets South Lamar, is Square Books, one of the finest independent bookstores in America and a temple to the written word, particularly of the Southern variety. From the second-story balcony along the side of Square Books, you can peruse a newly purchased paperback, sip a cup of coffee, perhaps do some writing if the spirit so moves you, or just gaze out onto the home turf of such local talents as Willie Morris and Barry Hannah.

The owner, Richard Howorth, who is usually on hand to greet customers and make reading recommendations, was once the mayor of Oxford. Admiring locals say he could have been mayor for life if he had wished, but his heart was in literature. He took a few moments out of a busy day to meet with me in his high-ceilinged upstairs office, whose walls are lined with first-edition works by some of the most distinguished of Southern authors.

"Square Books, is, I think, like any strong independent bookstore, rooted in its community," said the cardigan-wearing proprietor, leaning forward in his chair. Howorth seemed to be an ideal person to ask about a story I hoped to do in Oxford: how to raise literacy rates through good literature.

About 23 percent of the residents of Lafayette County, of which Oxford is the county seat, are functionally illiterate, according to the Lafayette County Literacy Council. It may come as a surprise to some who see Mississippi as a laggard in nearly every national measure, but the illiteracy rate for Lafayette County pretty much matches the national rate. The U.S. Department of Education has conducted large-scale assessments of adult proficiency in language in recent years. A study released in April 2002, said to be the most comprehensive study of literacy ever commissioned by the U.S. government, involved lengthy interviews with more than 90,700 adults statistically balanced for age, gender, ethnicity, education level and location (urban, suburban or rural) in 12 states across the United States. The survey, designed to represent the U.S. population as a whole, found that 21 to 23 percent of adult Americans were not "able to locate information in text," could not "make low-level inferences using printed material" and were unable to "integrate easily identifiable pieces of information." In other words, they were functionally illiterate.

"I think it's distressing there's such a high rate of illiteracy," Howorth said, "but I don't think it's a terribly big leap to go from being a very sort of basic reader, a crude reader, if you will, to a person who's able to read and quote 'literature.'"

High and fine literature is wine, and mine is only water; but everybody likes water.

—Letter to William Dean Howells, Feb. 15, 1887

Howorth invited me to that week's edition of Thacker Mountain Radio, broadcast live every Thursday night from Off Square Books on Van Buren Avenue, one of three buildings that comprise Square Books. The show goes out on Rebel Radio 92.1, serving northern Mississippi, and on Mississippi Public Broadcasting. I gladly accepted, and I soon found out that about half the town shows up for the show. As the place filled up, I spotted Bob and Jane Pekala and then Dr. O'Quin and her family taking their seats and waving my way.

The placard for that night's show said it would feature readings by authors Roy Blount Jr. and Jessica B. Harris. I did a backstage interview with the producer and was given a spot up front from where I could shoot video of the show. Host Jim Dees counted down from five to one – the cue for the house band, the Yalobushwackers, to kick off the evening.

Humorist Roy Blount Jr. read from his newly released book Alphabet Juice, on the peculiarities of language, and a poem that he called "An Ode to O":

O O, how empty yet how full

You are; how like the moon you pull.

You're just inside the door of *home*.

You calm us down when we say *Om*.

You couldn't be more in the middle of *now*.

If it weren't for you, we couldn't go "Wow!"…

Jessica B. Harris, a historian of culture and food, described the influence of "Mammy the house slave" on the food prepared by slaves for their owners and on the etiquette in the "big house." Much of Southern cuisine is derived from African recipes and techniques brought here by slaves, and those "yes, ma'ms" and "no, sirs" passed on by slaves to white children are still very much a part of Southern speech.

The audience, by this time spilling onto the sidewalk and the street, seemed to love every minute of the show, clapping and whooping approval.

Afterward, I cornered Ms. Harris, the author of numerous cookbooks and an expert on the Africanization of the Southern palate, and asked for her views on raising literacy rates.

"Oh, you've gotta read," she said, tilting her head toward me to be heard over the din of the crowd. "If you don't have the keys, you can't open the door. You should read anything and everything. It may be a cereal box if that's all you've got.

"But don't limit yourself," she went on. "I mean, I'm like a 2-year-old when I ride in the car or like a 4-year-old that's just learning how to read. I read the signs. I read the stores. I read the cereal boxes. I read everything. ... Everybody may not be ready to or want to read Faulkner. Read a graphic novel. Read a comic book. Read a newspaper. I keep sayin': Read the cereal box. Just read something – it will change your life."

Well, three or four months run along, and it was well into the winter now. I had been to school most all the time and could spell and read and write just a little, and could say the multiplication table up to six times seven is thirty-five, and I don't reckon I could ever get any further than that if I was to live forever. I don't take no stock in mathematics, anyway.

—*Adventures of Huckleberry Finn,* 1885, Chapter 4

Following Thacker Mountain's hour-long extravaganza, I was swept up into the local tradition of repairing to a nearby restaurant and upstairs bar called City Grocery, overlooking the Square. There I met Square Books devotees Michael Bible and David Swider and their 20-something friend, author John Brandon, writer-in-residence at Ole Miss. John's debut novel, *Arkansas,* had recently been published by McSweeney's, a San Francisco publishing house. He related that, after the publication, he received a phone call from Barry Hannah, who asked him to come to Oxford, where he would have the use of John Grisham's old house, a stipend and a position at the university as the John and Renee Grisham Writer-in-Residence. "I know you'll have to talk this over with the wife, so just let me know when you do," he quoted Hannah as telling him. To which he laughed and replied: "Christ, I can tell you right now the answer is yes!"

Michael and David told me about their newly launched literary magazine, *Kitty Snacks,* and I told the trio about my trip down the Mississippi and the stories I hoped to do in Oxford. After several rounds of Jack Daniels on the rocks and the occasional bottle of Reb Ale, John took me to another table to meet Roy Blount Jr., who agreed to be interviewed later that week.

———

My contact for a story about literacy and literature was the Lafayette County Literacy Council, whose building houses the local office of AmeriCorps VISTA, a national service program whose mission is to combat poverty. VISTA volunteers Nicole Bass and Sally Frederic told me they would be paying their first visit that day to a woman named Sherry Crocker, who had asked for help in learning to read. I was allowed to tag along.

It was raining as we drove from the city center in Nicole's Jeep Cherokee, all of us a bit nervous and excited about meeting a woman who was brave enough to admit she couldn't read and to ask for help. As the Cherokee made its way up a dirt path in an area of rolling green hills, we saw a ramshackle 1950s brick house, its roof in disrepair and the front door open. Sherry, a white woman in her late 30s, was visibly nervous about the whole idea, but she agreed to have the meeting recorded on camera because the video might encourage other people who couldn't read to seek help. This mother of two small boys invited us to sit at her kitchen table as she asked Nicole and Sally to help break the cycle of illiteracy in her family.

Roy Blount Jr. had taken time to talk to me earlier that week, and what he had said on the sounds and structure of language came back to me as I watched Nicole and Sally work with Sherry on sounding out the syllables of words.

"I've always believed that words are physical things," Blount had said, "that all English at some level is body English and that language is formed by the tongue and by other parts of the mouth. And that the more physical your writing is the more expressive it will be and the stronger it will be. So I looked into every letter of the alphabet and the sounds of it – the sound 'ch,' for instance, the combination of 'c' and 'h' – 'ch' – a hard 'ch' is a really catchy thing – that's why people say 'gotcha' and 'rock wichyou' and 'you betcha.' And I've always just loved focusing on the sounds of letters. … I think writing is best when it is in touch with speech. There's another 'ch' for you – speech."

Sherry was now going through a list of letters and their sounds prepared by Nicole and Sally. "A" makes the sound "aaah," she said, indicating the letter with her finger. "B" makes the sound "bbbb." But when she got to "h," she was stumped. "My name's got an 'h' in it," she said, scratching her ear and looking flustered. "And my little boy – his name starts with an 'h.'"

"Can you say his name?" Nicole asked.

"Yeah. Hunter."

"OK, and take that 'unter' off and what's that first sound?"

A long pause. "Ah," said Sherry, shaking her head. "I still have no idea."

Sherry said she wanted to be able to read so she could

help her 4-year-old with his schoolwork and to understand the notes he brings home from class.

Jon Scott, news editor for the Oxford Eagle, had told me earlier that what a child learns in school will frequently rub off on the parent. "It's catching, somehow or another," he said. "I've got three kids, and when a writer has come to read to the class, they come home and they tell me about it. And, you know, I can tell that they've been inspired. Certainly on that level it's very contagious."

Matching printed letters with the sounds they make in speech is, of course, a first step in mastering a language. But it's a long way from there to digesting and appreciating some of the fine literature produced in Mississippi. "Illiteracy to literature" was the theme for a story that I wanted to report on in Oxford. So I went back to Michael Bible and David Swider, the youthful progenitors of a new literary journal, to get some ideas.

I joined them for a beer at the Ajax Diner. Their passion for the written word turns nearly every conversation between the two into a brainstorming session about what would be cool to include in their journal, *Kitty Snacks*. At 25 and 28, respectively, David and Michael are relatively young to have launched a literary magazine. But their youth, they said, reinforces the lofty aim of *Kitty Snacks* – to make good writing accessible to people of all ages by offering it as bite-sized snacks.

We walked across the Square to Square Books, where upstairs we found a table and some cane chairs. The setting, with shelves full of books on the South and signed photographs of authors who had visited the store, couldn't have been more appropriate.

David and Michael showed me the first two editions of *Kitty Snacks* – a journal of graphic art, poetry and fiction. The editions contained some works by unknown writers and others by such nationally acclaimed authors as Leni Zumas, John Brandon and Kevin Wilson. "It's kind of different from most magazines in that it's got a very DIY feel to it – like you can see this and say, hey, man, maybe I could make one of those," David said. "A lot of times we publish people who have not been published before."

Wayne Andrews, executive director of Oxford's Yoknapatawpha Arts Council, talked in a separate interview about the difficulty of getting a book published in a stagnant economy and when more and more readers are choosing e-books rather than printed copies. He said he immediately saw the potential for Kitty Snacks and helped to get it published.

"The book is kind of a hard commodity right now," he said. "Publishers aren't taking risks on new authors nor publishing diverse works. We're finding new ways to do it." Quarterly publications like *Kitty Snacks,* he said, are "leading people down the path to discover a magazine and then hopefully to discover a book."

Speaking of his home state and the potential audience for his literary magazine, Michael called Mississippi "the fattest, poorest, dumbest state in the country – that is full of geniuses."

"You have people that can't read right next to people that win Nobel Prizes," he said. "And it's this weird kind of dichotomy that works to both illuminate that kind of difference but also, recently, to bring it together. And so, you kind of wonder what's the difference between William Faulkner and Muddy Waters, even though they were born very close to each other."

Blount had told me earlier: "I've talked to people who couldn't read and just faked it for years and years, and it must be a terrible pressure on people who are havin' to pretend to read for years and years. … It would be just so liberating to suddenly be able to actually do what you have been pretending to do. … The written word is a thing unto itself – different from the spoken word. It can carry the charge of the spoken word but it can also be better organized than the spoken word. It can go off in all directions that the spoken word can't quite do."

Michael ran his fingers through his hair, leaned forward and said: "There's literacy programs that will teach these ABCs and then, once that advances, then there's places that are gonna reach out with literature … and we want it to be interesting and fun."

Taking the first step toward becoming literate can be a daunting prospect for many adults who, in so doing, have to acknowledge they don't know how to read. There's a stigma attached to illiteracy.

"The mother's education is the most vitally important part of the child's education," Nicole said after her first lesson with Sherry. "The child, statistically, will have the same amount of education as the mother does. And the mother, especially in young children, is the No. 1 teacher. When mothers read to the children at home, when they help them with their homework, that's the most important part of a child's education. And in their upbringing, all the way through high school."

"Don't you give me none o' your lip," says he. "You've put on considerable many frills since I been away. I'll take you down a peg before I get done with you. You're educated, too, they say – can read and write. You think you're better'n your father, now, don't you, because he can't? I'll take it out of you. Who told you you might meddle with such hifalut'n foolishness, hey? – who told you you could?"

"The widow. She told me."

"The widow, hey? – and who told the widow she could put in her shovel about a thing that ain't none of her business?"

"Nobody never told her."

"Well, I'll learn her how to meddle. And looky here – you drop that

school, you hear? I'll learn people to bring up a boy to put on airs over his own father and let on to be better'n what he is. You lemme catch you fooling around that school again, you hear? Your mother couldn't read, and she couldn't write, nuther, before she died. None of the family couldn't before they died. I can't; and here you're a-swelling yourself up like this. I ain't the man to stand it – you hear? Say, lemme hear you read."

I took up a book and begun something about General Washington and the wars. When I'd read about a half a minute, he fetched the book a whack with his hand and knocked it across the house. He says:

"It's so. You can do it. I had my doubts when you told me. Now looky here; you stop that putting on frills. I won't have it. I'll lay for you, my smarty; and if I catch you about that school I'll tan you good. First you know you'll get religion, too. I never see such a son."

—*Adventures of Huckleberry Finn*, 1885, Chapter 5

Sherry's first reading lesson was intense and at times difficult. She had trouble picking out the consonant sounds on a page and pronouncing them. She was embarrassed, but determined not to give up. When asked why it might be scary for illiterate people to take the bold step she had taken that day, she beamed and said: "They're just scared. But me, I'm not scared at all. I'm enjoying learning how to read."

———

On Saturday, I met Dr. Jo Ann O'Quin to take part in Oxford's first annual Memory Walk to raise money for Alzheimer's research. It was a lovely, sun-splashed day for the walk, which began at the Ole Miss Lyceum and ended at the University Museum. Leading the procession in a University of Mississippi shuttle cart driven by Bob Pekala were Beth and Jay VanWinkle, the couple suggested by Dr. O'Quin as interviewees for a story about Alzheimer's. Beth had been diagnosed with Alzheimer's after her husband noticed that she would frequently lose her train of thought, had trouble balancing the checkbook and could no longer write coherently.

After the walk and reception, Jay, Beth and I piled into Jay's pickup and headed north to the town of Hernando, on Interstate 55 in the rolling hills of northern Mississippi. Beth had set a goal to accomplish three things on her "bucket list" before – as she put it – going "into her cave," a place where she would no longer recognize the people around her. She had already checked off the first two items on her list: meeting Morgan Freeman, her favorite actor and star of the 2007 film *The Bucket List*, and jumping out of an airplane in fulfillment of a lifelong dream, which she referred to as "skydiving into Alzheimer's." Now it was time to realize her third wish: to ride a horse.

I asked Beth why riding a horse for the first and last time was so important to her. Speaking slowly and finding it difficult to get out the words, she said, "I love all animals – but I wanted to, I wanted to ride."

As we pulled off the highway, I felt like I was reliving that day with Nicole and Sally when we drove to meet Sherry and were about to witness a watershed experience in a person's life. Judy Belue greeted us as we pulled up to the ranch's gabled main house. "How about wearing a cowgirl hat?" Judy said to Beth, positioning a big black hat just so on her head. The horse was a 22-year-old strawberry roan named Star, and Beth was led up to her to stroke the muzzle. "It feels like velvet, doesn't it?" Judy said. And Beth could only agree. "It does, it does," she said. "He's just so gentle."

Helped by Jay and Judy, Beth climbed up onto the saddle. And there she sat, pretty as a picture in the afternoon sun, ready to take her first horseback ride aboard a mild-mannered Tennessee walking horse.

"How do you feel, Beth?" I asked. "Happy!" she said, wearing a big grin under the cowgirl hat. "And what would you tell other people about the importance of living their dreams," I asked. There was no hesitancy in her reply: "I'd say, go for it. I do it every day."

Don't part with your illusions. When they are gone you may still exist, but you have ceased to live.

—*Following the Equator*, 1897, Chapter 59

As Star headed for the trail to give Beth her "bucket list" ride, I paused to savor the moment. Here was testimony to the strength of the human spirit, a woman living life to the fullest and making the most of every single day. I thought back to my first meeting with the VanWinkles earlier in the week. "Sometimes when we're talking about our life and what lies ahead," Jay had said, "we sometimes end it by saying, 'It's been a good ride,' but we're still ridin', aren't we, Mom.'" To which Beth had responded, "Yup, it sure has. We are, we are."

CHAPTER
LIFE LESSONS OF
THE DUGOUT CANOE
THIRTEEN

First light over Island 67,
Lower Mississippi River

T HE MISSISSIPPI RIVER EXPLOITS OF canoe
guru and guide John Ruskey have been featured
in *Southern Living, National Geographic* and *Outside*
magazines. But it was John's work with at-risk children of the
Mississippi Delta that intrigued me.

With a promise to greet me when I arrived in New
Orleans, Bob and Jane Pekala had driven me halfway across
Mississippi back to Clarksdale in the Delta, where I met up
again with John, my former host. Now John and I were in his
truck heading across the Mississippi River on the cantilevered

Helena Bridge to Helena, Ark., where I had landed my canoe several weeks before and was picked up by John.

"Helena is one of two river towns on the southern Mississippi that forms a natural levee wall – a bluff city," John said as we crossed the bridge on U.S. 49 linking Mississippi and Arkansas. "The other is Vicksburg, which you'll come across a bit farther down."

Downtown Helena, a thriving blues community in the 1940s and 1950s, had hard luck written all over it. Graffiti was scrawled on the walls of the 19th-century brick and wooden buildings along Main Street, most of them abandoned and boarded up. But John seemed oblivious to the squalor as we drove through nearly deserted downtown streets and onto a road facing the levee wall to the Helena location of the Quapaw Canoe Co.

John had been volunteering his time for more than a year with a local charter school in the Knowledge is Power Program, or KIPP, a national network of free, open-enrollment schools that aim to prepare kids for college. So when the principal phoned John and asked if it would be possible to transform a log into a dugout canoe as a class project, the answer, of course, was: "We'd love to do that."

John rolled back a metal security door to open his shop, housed in what used to be a warehouse, and flipped a series of switches. The industrial lights flickered on, illuminating brick and glass walls decorated with original artwork and banners for canoe trips. Paddles were propped up against a trio of already finished dugout canoes and, off to the side, surrounded by classroom chairs with seats of molded red plastic, was a gigantic log that once was the trunk of a cottonwood tree.

Then we were off to collect the students. The KIPP middle school was only a few blocks away, and upon arrival we were buzzed in. The principal gave me a quick tour of the school and showed me with great pride where the finished dugout canoe would be displayed. School was letting out for the day, the bell just audible over the chatter and clatter of the kids as they headed outside to jostle for position in the school bus line. Among our students in canoe-building that afternoon would be Jerome, Frederick, Brooklyn and Veronica, and we all walked together to John's levee-side shop.

"Today, we're going to be artists, we're going to be mathematicians, and we're going to be skilled carpenters," John told the students as he gathered them together for the twice-weekly class. He led them to the chairs surrounding their work-in-progress, a stout log, nearly three feet in diameter and about 13 feet long, that bore a few scrape marks from the previous class session.

"The first part is the artistic process, so take a seat and draw a picture of the log," John said. "There's no grade on this – it's just for your own creative process."

The children took out their notebooks and pencils and began to draw what they thought the log would look like as a canoe. Some drawings were of conventional canoes, with the hull curved upward at each end; others pictured canoes with prows adorned by animal heads. At some point, the kids will vote on what form the log will take. But for now, they were just throwing out ideas. I photographed the children as they worked and was amused to see that a couple of the students had drawn me into their pictures.

> No photograph ever was good, yet, of anybody – hunger and thirst and utter wretchedness overtake the outlaw who invented it! It transforms into desperadoes the meekest of men; depicts sinless innocence upon the pictured faces of ruffians; gives the wise man the stupid leer of a fool, and a fool an expression of more than earthly wisdom. If a man tries to look serious when he sits for his picture the photograph makes him look as solemn as an owl; if he smiles, the photograph smirks repulsively; if he tries to look pleasant, the photograph looks silly; if he makes the fatal mistake of attempting to seem pensive, the camera will surely write him down as an ass. The sun never looks through the photographic instrument that it does not print a lie. The piece of glass it prints it on is well named a "negative" – a contradiction – a misrepresentation – a falsehood. I speak feeling of this matter, because by turns the instrument has represented me to be a lunatic, a Soloman, a missionary, a burglar and an abject idiot, and I am neither.

—Letter to the Sacramento *Daily Union*, July 1, 1866

John Ruskey doesn't speak in sound bites. He speaks with

conviction, from the soul. Asked how art, education and the Mississippi River come together, he said:

"They come together with each paddle stroke you take. If you watch the way a paddle cuts through the water – it creates a double spiral on either side of it – and if you look at the shape of a classic canoe, it's almost the same shape you see created in the water as you're stroking the paddle. And that's the wonderful thing about the Mississippi River and any moving water, but on the Mississippi you see it more than any other body of water I've experienced. You see expressions of patterns, of life patterns – the very basic patterns that govern our life. You see them expressed, constantly being expressed and then recreated over and over again. And so it's actually there on the face of the water that you see all those things come together. One of our mottos here is that the river brings us together, and in that sense it literally does bring together education and canoes and art. They all come together as you're paddling the canoe."

John had already inspired my journey. In a note I received before I set out on my trip down the Mississippi, he wrote, "Every paddle stroke will bring you one stroke closer to the first lock and dam at Minneapolis-St. Paul, to the arch at St. Louis, to the French Quarter of New Orleans. Paddle Strong!" And when the wind picked up and my progress faltered, those words had guided and inspired me. Now his words were inspiring a younger generation in a different way.

The ultimate goal of his class was not only to hollow out the log and shape it into a canoe, but to paddle it across the Mississippi and back before it occupied a place of honor at the kids' school as a model of excellence and inspiration for generations to come.

Brooklyn, the youngest of the group at age 10, squirmed and smiled as she told me she liked the idea of "carving canoes." Thirteen-year-old Frederick, short, skinny and serious, said, "I just think it's fun to be in the water and to be around a natural life environment." Behind him, his classmates chipped away, learning how to wield an ax safely, scraping in turns with an adze and hand planes. I asked Frederick why it was important for him to be here. "To learn more about canoes, and maybe it can become a career for me one day," he said. "Carving skills, how to use an ax, and everything else. Like building skills."

As the kids worked, John constantly posed questions and encouraged the students to use the measuring tape and industrial ruler to find the answers. "We have geometry. We have pyramids. We have spheres. What other geometric shapes do we have?" he asked. "What is this, what is the log?"

"A cylinder?" ventured eighth-grader Jerome, the oldest of the lot, moving his arms in a circular motion.

Veronica, a small girl with big black-rimmed glasses and a take-charge attitude, was already extending the tape measure along the side of the log. One of the KIPP school's mottos was displayed on the back of her polo shirt: "THERE ARE NO SHORTCUTS." Jerome stood by, observing before asking, "Do we need the base and the height?"

"The base and the height," John confirmed, bending down to sketch the log with chalk on the cement floor. "Now, I want you to think about it, mathematically. We can be mathematicians in this. We have the dimensions."

"Diameter – 28 by 26 inches," called out Veronica and Jerome. They put the length at 153 inches, nearly 13 feet.

Everyone pondered the problem that John was creating on the floor.

"Do any of you have math tomorrow?" he asked.

Jerome raised his hand and said, "I teach."

"Really, you teach math?" John asked.

"I algebra teach," the boy said, smiling slightly and exuding confidence.

"Really? OK, well why don't you give this as a word problem to your class: Now the question is, I want you to think about how heavy is this log, number one. And how heavy do we want it to be? One cubic inch – cottonwood log equals? Let's just take a guess, for argument's sake. One cubic inch. How much is that gonna weigh?"

"Oh, that's small," Jerome thought aloud. "So that's gonna be like 20?"

"Twenty what?" John asked.

"Twenty grams?" Frederick suggested.

"Twenty grams, OK," John said. "Should we use that as a guess?" He scrawled the numbers in yellow chalk on the cement floor, next to the dimensions of the log: "1 cubic inch = 20 grams."

"Well, I don't know yet. It's got to be ciphered, and it ain't the easiest job to do, either, because it's over four million square miles of sand at ten cents a vial."

—*Tom Sawyer Abroad, 1894,* Chapter 11

"So, present that to your class. And the rest of you guys, ask your teachers if they can help out with this word problem that we have from our dugout canoe workshop, OK?"

"Yes, sir!" the class responded in unison.

"Alright, now let's go to work."

Frederick and Jerome, with John helping, dug metal hooks into the wood, and in union pushed the log over. "OK, now pull it out," John said. "OK, now ease it down."

I asked Jerome what he thought of Mr. Ruskey. "I think he's a very cool person," he said with a smile.

"We've worked with individual schools," John told me. "Individual students, individual groups of youth on different canoes. And every canoe we've actually built has involved some youth at some point in the process – just because it's fun to do.

"And you see those shining metal tools, shining in the sun – and bang, and boom," John went on, creating his own sound effects for the work. "It's an exciting kind of project. But this will be the first time that we've worked with one school to create one dugout, entirely for that school."

As the kids chipped away at the canoe with ax and adze under the supervision of a shop employee, John showed me the three completed dugouts – all different in size and appearance.

"We used to call this the King Beaver because the log looked like it was a big beaver face," John said. "But as I was carving it you can see King Beaver became something else. Some people see a rhino. Some people see a dog. I just think he's a river god of some sort."

The highly polished wood had at the front what appeared to be the head of a rhinoceros, with perked-up ears and clenched teeth. A series of what looked like fish gills extended along either side.

John walked me over to another canoe, painted bright blue and green. "This is the Water Ram," he said. The front of the canoe looked like a ram's head, with red lips and eyebrows and, again, clenched teeth. John rapped it with his knuckles and said, "It's well built – like a well-built carving tool, it has good sound. And the Ram is a cottonwood, 17½ feet. And this is Froggy," John said, pointing to a smaller dugout, which he also rapped for good measure.

"Our mission with Quapaw Canoe Co. is to share the beauty of the Mississippi River with the world," John said, "and the only way to do it, to really understand the beauty of the river – especially the Lower Mississippi because you can't get close to it in any other way – is to get in a vessel you can paddle, either a canoe or a kayak. So that's the reason we don't sell them. We build them to use. The further we get away from Mother Earth, the more bad decisions we make. So we're trying to bring more happiness to the world with that one mission statement – just by getting people on the river in canoes and kayaks."

> *I went along up the bank with one eye out for pap and t'other one out for what the rise might fetch along. Well, all at once here comes a canoe; just a beauty, too, about thirteen or fourteen foot long, riding high like a duck. I shot head-first off of the bank like a frog, clothes and all on, and struck out for the canoe. I just expected there'd be somebody laying down in it, because people often done that to fool folks, and when a chap had pulled a skiff out most to it they'd raise up and laugh at him. But it warn't so this time. It was a drift-canoe sure enough, and I clumb in and paddled her ashore.*

—*Adventures of Huckleberry Finn,* 1885, Chapter 7

Back at the canoe taking shape, John was quick with words of encouragement for the kids. "If you're removing wood, you're doing a good job," he told the class. "It's all about wood removal."

Veronica, the older of the two girls working on the project, paused to wipe her brow and massage her arm. She was all smiles as she spoke about her parents. "Yes, they're happy for me to be here today because they think if I can do something, then they can do it, too." I told her that Indians who lived on the river long ago had built canoes like the one she and her classmates were making. For them, too, it was a group effort.

By making this canoe for the school, she replied, "you'll have something to pass down from generation to generation, and everybody will know you and the thing that you made and how well you did. And how much effort you put into it."

It struck me that John wasn't only trying to expand his canoe business, but was also lending a hand to a struggling town by providing hands-on training to local kids and putting a few dollars into the pockets of the young "Mighty Quapaws in-training," as John called his youthful helpers.

Such a one was Shemiah Timberlake, who worked quietly in the background as the younger children began shaping the dugout canoe. He was one of the older kids who John employed in his shop and as river guides. I had met Shemiah when John had picked me up at Helena several weeks before. Though only 15, Shemiah spoke with the wisdom of a much older person – about the importance of family, about the wonders of nature, about preparing for college. Shemiah already had lived an eventful life. His family had survived Hurricane Katrina in 2005 and had moved to Clarksdale after the disaster.

"I remember being frustrated, sad, a little bit of scared," he said of the hurricane and its aftermath. "But I really was afraid for my little brothers, 'cause they were only little toddlers at that time, and it was hot and it's not really good for little babies."

I asked Shemiah about his work for John Ruskey at the Quapaw Canoe Co. "It gets us thinking," he said, tapping his forehead with his index finger. "We use our hands 'cause it gets us more into it, it lets us learn more about our heritage, our history, and everything like that. And also an education, 'cause a lot of us kids, we need that for our future." He swallowed hard, reflecting on his own remarks.

I found this attitude among most of the people I talked to on this stretch of the river. Reluctant to trumpet their hurts and fears brought on by hard times, they just pitch in to help those around them. And John Ruskey was looked to as one of those who provide help in times of need.

Over dinner with John, his wife and family on my last night in Clarksdale, I asked him about his reputation as one of the area's foremost experts on the river. He just laughed and told me about another "expert" further down the Mississippi at Vicksburg. "The 'expert' of Vicksburg went out one day and never came back," John said. "They never found a thing." His body, his canoe, his provisions were never seen again – as if he had become one with the river that had been his purpose in life.

I took a last, long walk around Clarksdale the next morning, loaded my gear into the canoe and pushed off from Quapaw Landing. It had been a month since I'd last been on the river, and the Mississippi was in a grumpy mood that day. I had to reacquaint myself with handling a small craft on a large expanse of choppy water. It was a humbling experience, and, recalling John's story about the "expert" from Vicksburg, I never for an instant took the Mississippi for granted.

Late in the afternoon, lost in my thoughts, taking turns between paddling hard and letting myself drift with the current, as John had instructed, I spotted a picture-perfect island in the middle of the river.

There was plenty of daylight left, but the island was too inviting. So I landed on the northern tip, dragged my canoe onto the sand, and, just for the heck of it, opened my laptop to see if I could get a wireless connection to check my email. The indicator showed two bars, some hope for a connection, so I paddled to the downriver end of the island and set up camp among some trees. But, alas, there was no signal at the campsite, so I made my way on foot back to the northern tip, sat down as the sun was setting and opened my MacBook. With just enough bars for a tenuous connection, I found a single email, sent from what appeared to be the account of the sister of an old friend named Sathyan.

I had wanted to share this adventure with Sath and we had hoped to meet somewhere before the end of my trip.

"I've been following your journey and wish I was there," Sath had written in an email from Dallas about a month earlier. "I'm pretty much tied up until the first week of November but will try to meet up after that. I was thinking of meeting up with you in Oxford, MS, for a few days or making the last leg of your journey into New Orleans. Any suggestions?"

Our meeting in Oxford didn't happen, so I looked forward to getting together with Sath in New Orleans to share a smile, a Johnny Walker and a beignet. I eagerly began to read the new email. But I was stunned by the news it bore: Sath had died suddenly in Texas on Oct. 30.

"Hello, as Sath's sister, I wanted to ensure that you knew of his untimely passing," the email said. "All the best, Chitra." Attached to the email was a copy of the program for Sath's funeral, which had already taken place, a photo of him smiling and an account of his too-short life written in the past tense.

I sat on that sandbar and cried. I couldn't believe it. I thought about Beth VanWinkle and how much time she had left before succumbing to Alzheimer's. I thought about my mom, about my brother, about so many others that were no longer among the living. Sath hadn't met me in Oxford because he had died before he could make it. I felt like a terrible friend for not having called to ask: What's up? Are you OK? Can we meet a bit farther down the river?

When I got down out of the tree I crept along down the river bank a piece, and found the two bodies laying in the edge of the water, and tugged at them till I got them ashore; then I covered up their faces, and got away as quick as I could. I cried a little when I was covering up Buck's face, for he was mighty good to me.

—*Adventures of Huckleberry Finn*, 1885, Chapter 18

I'd first met Sath Kandaswami at the Windsor Hotel in Cairo, Egypt, a few years earlier. We had both just arrived in Cairo and had struck up a friendship over breakfast. Sath had come overland from Morocco and I had flown in from Cape Town, South Africa.

Eager to explore Egypt, we bought tickets for a bus trip to Bahariya Oasis, in the Sahara Desert about 225 miles west of Cairo where we visited a frontier museum with mummies from Egypt's Greco-Roman period. In Bahariya, we hired a couple of Bedouin guides who took us into the desert where we camped out under the stars. The dunes of the Sahara stretch as far as the eye can see. Sath and I climbed to the top of a dune at sunset and surveyed that majestic desert.

Back in Cairo, we took an overnight train south along the Nile. I got off at Luxor and Sath went to the end of the line at Aswan. Sath eventually traveled on to Sudan, crossing the desert to Khartoum in a rented 4-by-4. I'd met up with Sath again in Washington, D.C., where we both worked for a time. It was there that we last shook hands and went our separate ways.

Now, as I sat on another sand dune, surrounded by an

expanse of water rather than sand, I had only fond memories of my friend Sath. I couldn't contact anyone from my campsite; the wireless signal was too weak to make a connection with my phone or laptop. I couldn't sleep that night as I tossed and turned, my mind roiling with memories of Sath. As the sun rose over the river the next morning, I got out of my tent and shouted to the heavens: "You could have been here … Look at this sunrise … You should have been here!"

That was when I realized I was a fool. As I stood looking out at the river, enjoying the first warmth of the rising sun, watching the water ripple as my island parted it on its journey to the sea, I thought of all those who had gone before – my mother, my brother, Dan Eldon, Sam Clemens and my friend Sath. I realized that I wasn't really alone. They were all smiling, right along with me. They were all here.

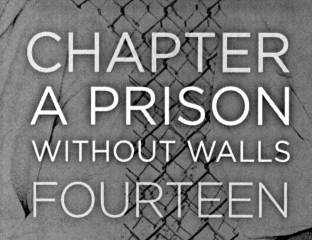

CHAPTER
A PRISON
WITHOUT WALLS
FOURTEEN

Aiming to better their lives,
at the Louisiana State Penitentiary

I HAD NO IDEA THAT ANGOLA has no perimeter wall. I canoed along the natural barrier that borders three sides of the once-notorious Louisiana State Penitentiary – the Mississippi River. It was dusk as I set a course for Shreves Bar Island, about a mile and a half downriver from the prison's ferry landing. I had passed the dock just after sunset and figured it would be the best way to get into the maximum-security prison the next morning.

I made camp on the sandy shore of Shreves Bar Island and crawled into my tent to work out a plan for the next day. I would awake at first light, shoot an introductory video for a story I planned to do on the prison, then paddle back upstream to the prison's ferry landing. I wouldn't be like other visitors who approach the main entrance from Louisiana 66. No, I would come in from the river and enter at the ferry landing.

The sun broke through the morning mist as I set up my introductory shot for a CNN piece on Angola, the largest maximum-security prison in the United States. Balancing my laptop computer with its built-in iSight camera on a gear bag, I knelt on the sand and used my canoe, the river and the prison as a backdrop.

"We're here on Shreves Bar Island in the middle of the Mississippi River, directly across from the largest state penitentiary in the United States – Angola State Penitentiary," I began, wearing several days' growth of beard, the breeze rustling my unkempt hair. "Once considered the bloodiest prison in America, Angola has dramatically turned itself around, thanks in great part to a mantra of communication under the positive leadership of Warden Burl Cain."

I wanted to shoot video as I paddled upstream, to document my entry into the prison grounds. But the Mississippi was running high and fast and my progress was slow. I was afraid that I'd be late for my first appointment, at 10 a.m., inside Angola. Forward progress was impossible in the center of the river, so I cut toward the shore, where

I could measure my headway against the willows and sycamores and the high-water debris along the riverbank. I had brought on my trip two identical paddles, both made by the Old Town Canoe Co. in the 1960s. To this point, I had used only one, and now it snapped in half.

With no way to control the canoe, it began to spin toward the overhanging limbs of a huge bois d'arc tree, all gnarled and twisted and looking like a monster about to ensnare me. I grabbed my backup paddle and finally made it to the ferry landing, where I dragged my canoe and gear onto the shore.

Nearly everything I knew about prisons was gleaned from the 1994 film *The Shawshank Redemption*. So I reckoned there might be a law against what I was about to do – paddle up to a maximum-security prison in a canoe, with a shotgun and a couple boxes of ammunition in one of my bags. I was a bit surprised when I didn't see anybody at all – no guards, no prisoners, no bloodhounds. I looked back toward my island and smiled. I'd made it.

But now, what to do with my heavy bags of gear and my canoe? As I dragged my belongings into the brush, a white pickup emblazoned with the letters "LSP" rolled up. The driver climbed out and walked onto the ferry landing, seemingly unaware of me. The man wasn't wearing anything that looked like prison garb, so I approached, a bit sheepishly, and called out, "Hello." He wheeled around and thrust out his hand in greeting, introducing himself as "trusty Charles

Martin." I introduced myself as a journalist, gestured to the dirt track he had driven along and asked how far it was to the prison gate. "What gate?" he asked with a puzzled expression.

I asked Mr. Martin if he might give me a lift. He shook his head no, and explained that he was a trusty, a "prisoner with privileges." But those privileges didn't extend to giving a ride to an unannounced stranger who pitched up at the ferry landing in a canoe. This was my first encounter with a "prisoner" at Louisiana State Penitentiary – a friendly, middle-aged man with a fine smile and a firm handshake. If he hadn't said he was a prisoner, I would never have guessed. He had no shackles, no striped uniform, no number, and there he was standing quite alone on the bank of the Mississippi River.

"Ah, here's a patrol truck now," Martin said, gesturing to a pickup identical to the one he had arrived in. We both waved at the truck and the uniformed female driver waved back.

"You know, most visitors come around the other side, from the road," she said once she had stepped down from her truck. When I pointed to my canoe, she nodded her understanding and talked to someone on her radio. I was scheduled to meet first with Vice Warden Cathy Fontenot. Once cleared, we went to get my gear.

"The bag the convict is loading into the truck contains a loaded shotgun," I whispered to the driver.

"Which one?" she whispered back. No alarm, no rebuke, no arrest on the spot. She didn't even flinch.

"The big blue one," I said. She shrugged an OK and said no more.

We drove away from the river and soon met another female guard, Maj. Joli Darbonne. We transferred my gear from one truck to the other and then were off to the "Ranch House," the prison's command center.

Louisiana State Penitentiary, sometimes called The Farm or the Alcatraz of the South, occupies 18,000 acres on some of the finest farmland in the southern United States. It has a staff of about 1,200 and about 5,100 inmates. The prison is large enough to have its own ZIP code – 70712.

The new guard was friendly and personable, explaining that she was with the media department and would be my guide for the day. I learned that about 200 families live on The Farm and that some members of staff families had parents who worked at the prison. Some staff members were even born here and would spend their lives working alongside the inmates.

As we drove toward the center of the prison complex, Maj. Darbonne pointed out a heavily fortified structure that houses Death Row and other maximum-security cellblocks. Along the road, we saw prisoners marching single file along a path with hoes over their shoulders, under the watchful eyes of armed guards on horseback. I asked for permission to snap a photo, and my guide said it was OK. She explained that some of the cotton, cabbage, corn, okra, and other crops grown on The Farm, as well as meat from the cattle, is sent out of the prison for sale. This, she said, was partly to appease local politicians who want the prison to be self-sustaining.

Warden Burl Cain, credited with introducing reforms that have improved conditions and reduced violence at the prison, has been afforded the freedom to try a series of innovative projects, such as an inmate-run radio/TV station. This was the focus of the story I planned to report on at the prison: the role of communications in the inmates' daily lives and how it affects their attitudes toward long-term incarceration. In Louisiana, a sentence of "life in prison" means "life in prison."

The road cut left and we pulled up to the Ranch House, a tree-shaded, mid-20th-century bungalow that houses the offices of the warden and the vice wardens. A giant of a man with polite manners and an educated tongue introduced himself as "Big Lou" and helped me unload my canoe from the truck. He told me that he loved CNN's "Morning Express with Robin Meade" and asked if I had ever met her. I told him no, but that I had once filed a report from China that landed on her program. Big Lou was impressed and took extra care with my canoe as he helped me position it on a padded boat trailer before leading me to the Ranch House's dining hall.

As we walked, another man introduced himself as an assistant warden and asked softly what I thought about the big man who had helped me with my canoe. "He's a nice and bright guy, awfully friendly," I reported, to which theassistant warden said, "The man is a convicted killer. He's a trusty, which means we give him a level of trust and respect and free rein, because of his good behavior." I looked toward Big Lou and he smiled, as if to say, ah shucks. "I made a mistake, a big mistake, and I'm paying my debt to society," Big Lou said, shaking my hand. "I'm living proof it's possible to be rehabilitated."

Maj. Darbonne and I took seats near the head of a table in the dining hall. Other prison honchos filtered in, took seats, sampled the freshly pickled vegetables served as appetizers and asked about the canoe outside. The assistant wardens seemed to defer to a stocky, blond kid barely into his 20s who was particularly interested in my canoe. I would learn later that he was the warden's youngest son. He asked me to relate some of the high points of my trip down the Mississippi, and an assistant warden told me that the young man would probably like to undertake such a journey himself. "I couldn't do it, even if I wanted to," the young man said, telling me he'd just signed on for a different kind of adventure: marriage. I thought of the more memorable parts of my trip so far and mentioned my time on the Koether Ranch in northeastern Iowa. The young man grinned and said he had had a similar experience on a cattle ranch in Colorado, working with cowboys and horses and camping out on the range.

The boss, Warden Cain, walked in, took his seat at the

center of the table and lunch was immediately served. "What brand of firepower are you carrying?" asked a vice warden during the meal. I told him about the .410 shotgun, given to me by Greg Koether in Iowa, and the assembled wardens nodded in approval. "I'd say you'd be a damned fool not to carry a weapon on this river," the warden said, summing up the consensus at the table. For a moment I felt like a bad-ass dude, talking about my Snake Charmer shotgun and surrounded by jailers. But I didn't tell them that I probably would never fire the weapon, even to save my life.

The joke of these highwayman friends of ours was mainly a joke upon themselves; for they had waited for me on the cold hill-top two full hours before I came, and there was very little fun in that; they were so chilled that it took them a couple of weeks to get warm again. Moreover, I never had a thought that they would kill me to get money which it was so perfectly easy to get without any such folly, and so they did not really frighten me bad enough to make their enjoyment worth the trouble they had taken. I was only afraid that their weapons would go off accidentally. Their very numbers inspired me with confidence that no blood would be intentionally spilled. They were not smart; they ought to have sent only one highwayman, with a double-barrelled shot gun, if they desired to see the author of this volume climb a tree.

—*Roughing It*, 1872, Chapter 79

I asked about their own firepower, and other means to

keep the trusties from escaping by jumping into the river or making a dash for the nearby Tunica Hills. The vice warden in charge of chase dogs said escape attempts were rare, but occasionally did occur.

"It happened the other month," he reported. "One we'd never have suspected of skipping out – an old-timer. And he didn't do it by the river, per usual. He ducked and waited and took his time, running over the hills."

"When this happens," said Cain, "every single guard picks up a gun, even Maj. Darbonne here. And the inmates respect what we've gotta do. We put them all in lockdown and we go out and search, and keep searching, until we find and apprehend the runaway at large."

The whole lot of us gathered in the warden's office for a post-lunch interview session, even the warden's son, who declared: "I'm normally not interested in this sort of thing, but this interview I do want to hear." With an audience of 10 to 15 prison officers who sat on chairs brought into the office, I orchestrated the interview. I first asked the warden to pose for a photo and then began asking questions.

"Warden Cain, for the 86 percent of prisoners who are never going home, and who know they are never going home, how are you able to offer them hope?"

The white-haired warden, who packs a few extra pounds and has the look of an outdoorsman, launched into a definition of *hope*: mainly a belief in a god or an afterlife.

"Everybody believes in something," he said. "If we can get focused on later rather than now, then we can do the time … Though you may be here all your life, let's not let here be so oppressive that you can't be here without violence. … And then let's have hope that when we do pass on to the next world, that we receive the blessing of being good here."

I asked about his innovations in communications and if that gives the inmates a feeling that they have some say in their everyday lives.

"We have our own TV station, and we have our own radio station," he said. "The radio station is the way I communicate with the inmates, but also the radio station is the way they communicate with each other, which like any radio station in the city, would be beneficial. So we get the same benefit here."

He said the TV station has an added benefit. "It trains inmates in that skill, so if they ever are released from prison, then they'll be employable," the warden said.

"That's part of the rehabilitation. I can teach you to be moral, but I also have to teach you how to read and write and give you skills and trades. Now if I give you all that without morality, I just made a smarter criminal. It all goes together. So everything you see here is a learning experience for the inmate so they have skills if they do get out, that they can contribute. Plus, they contribute to the community here."

I learned during my day with the officers and inmates that the means of communication introduced by Cain have, in effect, broken down a wall that had existed between the prison hierarchy and the lowly con. With a prisoner-run magazine and broadcast stations, suggestions can be made on how to improve conditions; grievances can be aired before they fester into violence. And the inmates seemed to be genuinely appreciative.

One such man was Richard Vinet, 54. He was not on Death Row, but he was very near the end of his life. Vinet had been placed in the hospice's "vigil" room, the place where the doctors assign inmates who are believed to have fewer than 24 hours to live. I had been ushered past security and through hospital doors to the hospice, where, I was told, about 35 Angola inmates die of natural causes every year. The hospice had about 10 beds and was much like a nursing home in the outside world. Some inmates were on oxygen and dozing in their beds; others were rolling about in wheelchairs.

> *That same day several prisoners were brought in to remain over-night, who were being conveyed, under guard, to various places in the kingdom, to undergo punishment for crimes committed. The king conversed with these – he had made it a point, from the beginning, to instruct himself for the kingly office by questioning prisoners whenever the opportunity offered – and the tale of their woes wrung his heart.*

—*The Prince and the Pauper*, 1882, Chapter 27

I photographed Bibles, canisters of oxygen and loaves of bread, and then was admitted into the "vigil" room. Vinet was propped up in his bed, his skin a sickly yellow color and his beard and frizzled hair a dirty white. A photographer from *USA Today* was also at the prison for a visit that day, and he joined me in the "vigil" room. He snapped photos as I took a chair and began to talk to Vinet. I hadn't expected to be put into this position, so I kept my questions basic.

"How long have you been at Angola, and what would you most like to say?" I asked.

"Since '84, I think. Since 1984," he said, stroking his beard, deep in thought. And then, in what served as a final testimony, he said: "I'd like to thank Burl Cain and, and that radio station, and the little program that he has. Yeah."

It was simple and moving. I could think of no more questions to ask this man whose death was imminent. I breathed deeply, shook Vinet's hand and departed, escorted by Maj. Darbonne.

Just down the walk from the hospital, she ushered me into the gospel sounds of KLSP Radio.

The "trusty" disc jockey at the radio station sported a neatly shaved goatee, a blue denim shirt, a fancy watch and a teardrop tattoo under one eye. As the gospel tune came to a close, he put on his headphones and pulled the suspended microphone up close to his mouth.

"Alright, fellas, you're listening to KLSP radio station, 97.1 FM – the incarceration station, the only one in the nation," he said in his best radio voice. "You've been listening to the sounds of Yolanda Adams and she's saying, Someone Watchin' Over You. God bless you. Keep it locked right here at 91.7 for the very best in sermon and sound – KLSP."

When the next song began, the man snatched off his headset and, with his fingers still expertly on the controls, turned to face my camera.

"My name is Keith Alexander, I'm a deejay here at KLSP, and our motto is: 'We're the only incarceration station in the nation, the one that kicks behind the bricks.'

"We're on the air 24 hours a day," he continued in a voice smooth and compassionate. "We broadcast live all over The Farm here at Angola. It's a very personal radio station for the prisoners here. Anybody that has a transistor radio with headphones, whether you're in a dormitory, cellblock, whether you're on Death Row – or, as we like to call it, Live Row – you can tune in to KLSP all day and tune into some very good gospel music and your favorite deejays.

"As a prisoner myself, I live down the walk with the other guys, so these guys know me personally," Alexander said. "I've got a personal relationship with all of them, so most of the times, when I'm coming to work, even when I get off, they'll tell me, 'You know, Keith, tomorrow, could you play my favorite song?' As you'll notice, we've got a telephone here. Inmates aren't allowed to call, but what they're allowed to do is get the officer in the dormitory to call by way of our telephone and request their favorite song. So it's very personal.

A guy might be going through a situation, and he might want to hear a particular song, so he can have the officer call and request his favorite song, and I'll play that song and even call out his name and dedicate it to him personally.

"For me, personally, the radio station has allowed me to realize that there's always hope that you can be a better person no matter how dire your situation is. As a prisoner, I had no idea I had all this talent inside of myself. But good behavior is rewarded with a good opportunity to progress in life … And I think it goes to show you that a bad situation or a bad choice you make is not the end of the road. It's never too late to turn your life around, no matter what you do, no matter what you're faced with. There's always hope, there's always light at the end of the tunnel."

The gospel show resumed and Maj. Darbonne led me down the walk, into Cellblock D. The heavy steel doors clanked loudly, first in front of us and then behind us, as we entered the cellblock. We were headed for the prison's television station when we happened upon two young inmates who agreed to an impromptu interview.

"My name's Marlo Twain Green, and I've been here four years and three months," said the smaller of the two, both wearing matching gray hoodies. I asked about communications, through the magazine and the broadcast stations. "You have to reach out to people, to get help," he said. "If you don't, you'll just be stuck in here. And I'm young."

I panned to his bigger friend.

"My name's Devon Morris. I've been at Angola five years," he said, and then added, somewhat surprisingly: "I love it. I mean before I came to Angola I was in some sticky situations, but I'd rather be up here to do my time. "Twenty-three years old," he went on. "I've been here, been locked up since I was 17. That's why we just moved up here, for education, to get our education trades, different types of certificates to show that we better our lives. And other places, you don't got all these school programs, or religious programs, you know, nothin'. You're just in here."

He recalled his experience at another Louisiana prison before coming to Angola: "Just sittin' down. It feels like you just dyin'. But up here you've got something you can do, or you can interact with different sources of people, you know. I love it."

Both men had started the interview with suspicious stares. Now they were smiling.

I was led into a makeshift television station housed in one small room and run by journalistic novices Matthew Morgan and Shawn Vaughn. This was LSP/TV 21, and both men were trusties. One of their privileges is to occasionally travel to other Louisiana prisons to gather news.

"Well, this is very unique," said Vaughn, a middle-aged black man at the controls of a video-editing machine, as he took a break from editing "The Legal Forum," a show that offers legal advice to the inmates.

"I don't think there is anything like this in the world — a television station in a prison. Maybe on a small scale, but we do a lot of work around the state. And other inmates in the prison, it inspires them to keep their noses clean. They see us doing what we're doing, and they would like to be a part of it one day, and they know they have to make changes."

I again raised my standard question on communications in the prison. Vaughn leaned back, smiled and asked where he should start.

"Communication is important. Positive communicationis even more important," he began. "Dissemination of infor-mation — it makes for a peaceful environment, in my opinion.

"We're not animals; we're people here. And, yes, some of us have made mistakes, but people have made changes and have made improvements, and that's the side that the outside, that the media needs to see. They need to get that out to people because people have this — I like to say — 'Prison Break' view of prison.

"Warden Cain's made a plethora of changes in the prison. Also, some people here — the men who have decided that 'I don't want to go in the wrong direction anymore' — they've come to the conclusion that that doesn't work. And so they've made changes within themselves. And no matter what warden you have or what security you have, it's the individual that has to make the change. And we here at the television station, we've made changes in our lives and it's paid off."

From the TV station we paid a visit to the office of the

prison magazine, The Angolite, which has been published continuously since 1979.

> *I believed I had made a discovery — the discovery already indicated — the discovery of the wide difference in interest between "news" and "history;" that news is history in its first and best form, its vivid and fascinating form; and that history is the pale and tranquil reflection of it.*

—*Mark Twain's Autobiography*, page 283

At The Angolite, the tables were turned. The staff wanted to ask me questions for a story about an itinerant canoeist visiting the prison. The oldest inmate journalist introduced himself as Lane.

"Is this your first time in a prison?" he asked, notebook and pencil in hand.

"Yes, it is."

"What, may I ask, did you expect to find? Did you expect us to have horns?"

I looked to Maj. Darbonne for guidance, and she nodded that it was OK for me to answer.

"I think that all people, myself included, are both good and bad," I said. "That it's important to focus on the good, to encourage the good. And that's what I'm doing here today, what I've been doing my entire canoe journey down the Mississippi – looking for and finding positive American stories."

The tattooed assembly grinned and nodded, indicating that my answer passed muster. Now it was my turn to ask questions. But first I asked them to introduce themselves:

Kyle Hebert, religion writer, 44, incarcerated at Angola for nine years of a life sentence for attempted murder; Kerry Myers, editor, 53, in Angola for 19 years of a life sentence for murder; and Lane Nelson, managing editor, 55, in Angola for 28 ½ years of a life sentence for murder.

Myers, a tall, lanky, good-natured fellow, wore a T-shirt that said "Human Relations Club – Angola." He led off the discussion:

"Well, it's our job, it's our editorial mission to inform and educate. We have an audience here inside the prison and we see that as important, but not any less important than the subscriber base that we have that goes outside. We go to every state. We go to six foreign countries. A lot of our paid subscribers are media, academia, legal professionals, law libraries, courthouses, criminal justice classes, criminal justice editors. That's important – communication. And what we do is tell what a lot of mainstream media won't tell, or maybe have no interest in. And that's the real story – of who's who in prison, what prison is like and the policies that affect people – because you eventually pay for it."

Lane Nelson, the managing editor, was the most senior of the staff, working for The Angolite since 1993. He stepped forward, a cowboy belt holding up his Levis, his Louisiana State

Penitentiary T-shirt neatly tucked in. "What it gives to us, to do this, is meaning and purpose in an otherwise meaningless environment," he said. "And there are so many things now in Angola that a guy can latch onto to get up. He gets up in the morning, and he doesn't have to think to himself, 'I'm no closer to going home than the day I was arrested.' Instead, he can think about the purpose that's ahead in that day, whether it be the guy working on the range crew or whatever. And I think that has a lot to do with how the violence has decreased so much in this prison."

"The easiest thing for a warden to do is say no," added Myers. "It costs him nothing. It doesn't cost his staff any effort when he says no, but when he says yes, everybody else is responsible for doing something. So, yes, there's risk involved. Not to public safety – because the risk don't go outside the prison – but risk to careers, risk to reputation. ... So, when you invest, it's about investing in the quality of life. Maybe that's part of what we do here, too. I mean, we're invested in what we do, but we also get that message out. We're telling that story of how these people take that opportunity and what they do with it."

The religion writer, Kyle Hebert, confirmed that remark with an "Amen." And he launched into a tribute to Warden Cain that was more sermon than statement.

"He sees us as human beings, and I've heard him say often how he understands that the greatest gift an individual can acquire is his ability to communicate properly, and that's what he allows us to do, freely," Hebert said. "He allows us to live a life inside the walls of our consequences. Some of us – I can't speak for everybody – have committed crimes. But for that, in spite of what the judge has said, or the DA has said, here at Angola, Warden Cain allows us to live a life, productively, that not only helps ourselves out, but helps the community."

I thought back to the warden, who had surprised me by saying at the end of our interview, "I commend CNN for sending out someone like you, or for you coming out and telling it and explaining back to America, 'cause America's got to listen to these programs and realize it comes down to morality."

The day had rolled by so quickly I hadn't noticed that the sun was sinking toward the western horizon.

I hopped back into Maj. Darbonne's LSP pickup, hoping to make it to the prison's Point Lookout Cemetery before the sun set. As we drove to the final resting place for many of Angola's inmates, I thought of Richard Vinet, gasping for breath in the hospice "vigil" room, and telling me that his bad liver was the reason he'd be headed soon to Point Lookout. With a shaking index finger, he had pointed to the nurse in the corner and to Vice Warden Cathy Fontenot standing beside her. "I want to thank these two women here," he had said. Besides the radio station and his request for a final song, it was the people who were with him at the very end that made all the difference. "No inmate in this prison dies alone," Fontenot said.

> *The Impartial Friend: Death, the only immortal who treats us all alike, whose pity and whose peace and whose refuge are for all – the soiled and the pure, the rich and the poor, the loved and the unloved.*

—Mark Twain's last written words, to
  Albert Bigelow Paine, 1910

Cain takes a similar approach with the men on Death Row – "his children," he calls them. He holds their hands as they are executed by lethal injection. Nobody who dies here dies alone.

Now I stood at the wrought-iron gates of the old cemetery, bathed in the waning yellow light of the setting sun, and gazed at row upon row of white wooden crosses. This is the place where about a third of those incarcerated here will be buried because they have no family or friends to claim their remains. I walked among the crosses and found a bronze marker for the "unknown buried here." It bore this dedication: "Remember not my name nor my sins nor guilt nor shame; only that I was a man."

Later, two trusties helped me launch my canoe into the Mississippi. The sun had gone down, and the river's surface was a shiny black, reflecting the lights of a crew boat that was ferrying a shift of guards to the other side. Although I couldn't see it, I knew exactly where my island lay, having approached the night before under similar conditions. There comes a time on this river when you become one with your craft, when danger is outweighed by a sense of calm. The inmates who helped me launch, whose names I had forgotten to ask, waved and wished me Godspeed. A sliver of the moon broke momentarily through the clouds as the current took me. I waved back, feeling a camaraderie with the prisoners and their warden, but thankful to be free.

MAKE IT
RIGHT NOLA
FIFTEEN

*On the Lower Mississippi en route
to New Orleans*

Old Town

T HE TORTUOUS COURSE of the Mississippi River is measured by a series of mile markers. From the point where the Mississippi trickles out of Lake Itasca in northern Minnesota, it is about 1,347 river miles to Mile 0, where the Mississippi meets the Ohio River at Cairo, Ill. That's the end of what the U.S. Army Corps of Engineers calls the Upper Mississippi. From Cairo, along the Lower Mississippi, the mile markers begin anew. They count down from Mile 954 at Cairo to another Mile 0 at a place called Head of the Passes, where the Mississippi empties into the Gulf of

Mexico, about 95 miles downriver from New Orleans.

As I left Angola at Mile 265 and headed for Mile 234 at Baton Rouge, where the river is sufficiently wide and deep to accommodate huge, seagoing oil tankers and container ships, I realized my journey was nearly over. But I didn't want it to end. As I paddled hard to stay out of the way of the increasing number of ships and towboats, I wished I were back at Lake Itasca, just starting out on this splendid adventure.

I wanted to savor one last island campsite, and I found a nice one in a wide, lazy bend of the river not far from Baton Rouge. During the hour before sunset, I explored the edges of the island and found in the sand the fresh tracks of a bobcat. The island had a luxuriant growth of brush and trees, including cypress and cottonwood, and offered many sheltered spots for a campsite. I pitched my tent in a small clearing that was hidden from view in all directions, but I could just peek out at the river through a curtain of dewberry bushes, Virginia creepers, wild grapes and poison ivy. It was late November, apparently hunting season. No sooner had I set up camp than I heard a bugle somewhere along the riverbank, followed by the baying of hounds. But I was safe and out of sight in my leafy refuge.

At first light, I filmed a huge towboat pushing a seven-by-seven cargo of shipping containers downriver. And then, plowing upriver, was a gargantuan oil tanker with its name painted so high on the hull that I couldn't read it. I had had some close encounters with towboats and their barges further up the Mississippi, but now I was sharing the river with the really big boys. From the bridge of one of these giant vessels, my canoe would be barely visible. I reminded myself to be extra careful from here on out.

Of course, on the great rise, down came a swarm of prodigious timber-rafts from the head waters of the Mississippi, coal barges from Pittsburgh, little trading scows from everywhere, and broad-horns from 'Posey County,' Indiana, freighted with 'fruit and furniture' — the usual term for describing it, though in plain English the freight thus aggrandized was hoop-poles and pumpkins. Pilots bore a mortal hatred to these craft; and it was returned with usury. The law required all such helpless traders to keep a light burning, but it was a law that was often broken. All of a sudden, on a murky night, a light would hop up, right under our bows, almost, and an agonized voice, with the backwoods 'whang' to it, would wail out —

'Whar'n the ----- you goin' to! Cain't you see nothin', you dash- dashed aig-suckin', sheep-stealin', one-eyed son of a stuffed monkey!'

Then for an instant, as we whistled by, the red glare from our furnaces would reveal the scow and the form of the gesticulating orator as if under a lightning-flash, and in that instant our firemen and deck-hands would send and receive a tempest of missiles and profanity, one of our wheels would walk off with the crashing fragments of a steering-oar, and down the dead blackness would shut again. And that flatboatman would be sure to go into New

Orleans and sue our boat, swearing stoutly that he had a light burning all the time, when in truth his gang had the lantern down below to sing and lie and drink and gamble by, and no watch on deck. Once, at night, in one of those forest-bordered crevices (behind an island) which steamboatmen intensely describe with the phrase 'as dark as the inside of a cow,' we should have eaten up a Posey County family, fruit, furniture, and all, but that they happened to be fiddling down below, and we just caught the sound of the music in time to sheer off, doing no serious damage, unfortunately, but coming so near it that we had good hopes for a moment. These people brought up their lantern, then, of course; and as we backed and filled to get away, the precious family stood in the light of it – both sexes and various ages – and cursed us till everything turned blue. Once a coalboatman sent a bullet through our pilot-house, when we borrowed a steering oar of him in a very narrow place.

—*Life on the Mississippi*, 1883, Chapter 10

This last stretch of my journey – from Baton Rouge to Mile 95 at New Orleans – would be a challenge. It is notoriously hazardous for a canoeist. The river traffic is fierce and the boat captains hostile.

Back on the river for the penultimate day of my journey, I paddled long, hard and fast, trying to eat up enough of the remaining distance so that my final day would be short and easy. I continually scanned the horizon for big ships, but when

I would see one it was impossible to tell at first whether it was coming or going. Some of the vessels were anchored in the river, waiting for a berth to unload or take on cargo. Whenever I spotted a tanker under way, I'd paddle as fast as I could to the far side of the river. But sometimes another tanker would appear and I'd have to shoot down the center of the channel, right between them.

At one point, I had no idea which way to go. The current was carrying me along at a mighty clip, and ships and towboats were moving about in every direction. I chose to pass closely by a tanker anchored to my left. But as I shot forth, paddling like my life depended on it, a towboat made a beeline from the opposite side of the river, headed directly toward me. I couldn't stop my forward progress, so I tried to slow down. The towboat pilot apparently spotted me and slowed down, too, so I shot forward again, paddling strongly. Just then, a red Army Corps of Engineers patrol boat interfered. It came out from behind the tanker, cutting between my canoe and the approaching towboat in an apparent effort to ward it off. The patrol boat had come out so quickly and with such power that its wake nearly capsized the canoe. I rode a tidal wave of terror, thrust sharply upward and then down, all the while thinking that my time was up. I still don't understand how my canoe survived. My heart beat so fast for the next couple of hours that I felt physically ill. I knew that going into the water here would be almost certain death. The towboat pilots who didn't scream at me simply ignored me. I was a crazy solo canoeist, a nonentity, and, dead or alive, the least of their worries.

I wanted to make my last camp as close to New Orleans as possible, hoping to have only about 20 miles to paddle on the last day. But it turned out to be closer to 35. As I came to a halt at a turn in the river just as the sun was setting, a sudden headwind pushed me backward. At my left, a fleet of tows had shut down for the night, so I cut in behind them. I was sure this place was private property and might be protected by a guard dog, but I didn't care. I was tired and frazzled and needed some sleep. I made camp on a sandy embankment six inches above the river, keeping most of my gear packed and ready in the canoe, and set my alarm for 3:45 a.m.

I knew that I'd still be facing that headwind if I set out at first light. So I decided to try my luck paddling in the early morning darkness. I figured I'd snatch a couple hours' sleep, get back onto the river, paddle by the light of the moon while the boat traffic was less intense and try to make up for the time I lost the day before.

I awoke with my alarm and loaded the canoe, putting a lantern at the prow. With another light affixed to my cap, I pushed off and started to paddle, hugging the shoreline. There was, indeed, less traffic at night. I had paddled along for about an hour and a half, encountering no problems, when a towboat captain hailed me with a bullhorn and invited me to breakfast in his wheelhouse. It was still dark and starting to rain, so I called back, "Sure." The first mate threw me a line.

The captain was a short Creole, cocky as sin. He wore a crumpled black hat and a gold earring in his left earlobe. He told me he liked my "goddamned lights" and that he had seen me coming from far upriver. He was full of backhanded compliments – to me, to the first mate, and to the towboats that pushed past as we spoke. The river, he said, "separates the men from the boys," but he added that I "was attempting suicide with every paddle stroke I took." He said his family had worked the Mississippi for three generations. Then suddenly he started screaming and cussing at the skipper of a beautiful white towboat that cut through the morning mist like a specter, an American flag and another with a skull and crossbones flying high above the deck. I realized it wasn't personal when a towboat captain spewed invective. The f-word was, in fact, part of their preferred greeting.

This was a red rag to the bull. He raged and stormed so (he was crossing the river at the time) that I judge it made him blind, because he ran over the steering-oar of a trading-scow. Of course the traders sent up a volley of red-hot profanity. Never was a man so grateful as Mr. Bixby was: because he was brim full, and here were subjects who would TALK BACK. He threw open a window, thrust his head out, and such an irruption followed as I never had heard before. The fainter and farther away the scowmen's curses drifted, the higher Mr. Bixby lifted his voice and the weightier his adjectives grew. When he closed the window he was empty.

You could have drawn a seine through his system and not caught curses enough to disturb your mother with.

—*Life on the Mississippi*, 1883, Chapter 6

Even though he berated me, saying I was "lucky to be on his vessel," the skipper gave me use of his captain's chair, his personal porcelain bowl and the last of the cereal and milk.

Considering that I didn't want to drown on the last day of my trip, I ventured to ask about protocol in heavy river traffic. What am I supposed to do, I asked, if I come face to face with a towboat?

"You're supposed to talk it out on the radio," he said. "Every time you see another craft, you're supposed to suss out who goes where. When you approach one head-on, what you gotta do is cut away, well, well in advance, so they can see you, which direction you've decided."

When I told him I didn't have a radio, he replied, perhaps with a touch of sarcasm: "You don't have a VHF marine-band radio? That's just fine, 'cause these captains don't wanna talk to you anyhow!"

He told me to keep to the middle of the river whenever possible, because along this stretch of the Mississippi most of the action takes place close to shore. If I did have to cut toward the bank, he said, stay away from the tied-up barges on either side of the river because the current sweeping alongside the barges can be treacherous.

"People think they can swim to a barge and grab onto it before getting sucked under, but it don't work like that," he said. "The power of the river sucks you under regardless and traps you underneath. Certain, utter death."

I had hoped that the wind and rain might abate, but the weather only became nastier as I visited aboard the towboat. Back on the river, I made only 20 to 25 miles before the wind blew me to the right, directly to a Dow Chemical plant. I tied up to a shivering sycamore at the side of the plant, hoping it would offer some shelter. My hands shook crazily as I tried to tie a jacket to a branch to form a makeshift shelter, but the wind blew it loose no sooner than I had secured it. Fearing I was near to hypothermia, I stayed by the tree for about an hour trying to recover my faculties. But determination to get to the boardwalk at the French Quarter overcame my better judgment and I got back into the canoe. As I waited near the plant for an opening between a procession of tankers and towboats, a man in a white hardhat at the plant saw me struggling in the current. Cupping his hands to his mouth, he shouted, "What's you doin'?" I yelled back, "Headed downstream!" To which he shook his head and shouted back, "Good luck!"

Despite strenuous efforts to get back into the channel, where I could make some downriver headway, the wind kept pushing me toward the shore. I had little to no control of the canoe, and I decided: Well, this is the end of the line. It was a few miles short of the French Quarter, my intended final destination, but it would have to do. I stopped paddling and the wind blew me directly back toward the plant, alongside a wooded area enclosed by a chain-link fence. Along the fence at regular intervals were signs that said: "Private Property – Absolutely No Unauthorized Access – You Will Contract Cancer."

I phoned my friends Bob and Jane Pekala, who had just left Oxford, Miss., for the drive to New Orleans, where they had planned to meet me in the French Quarter. The rain was still blowing sideways and the folks in the plant, who must have thought I was an industrial spy, offered me no shelter. So in the pelting rain I dragged my canoe and all my gear onto the slope of the levee. I had told Bob of my predicament and where to find me on the levee road. So I had nothing to do for three hours but wait for Bob and Jane in the wintry rain, shaking myself silly. I finally spotted their vehicle approaching from far down the river road and wanted to wave, but I could no longer feel my hands and arms. My friends stepped out into the rain to help me with my gear and to give me a hug, and from that moment I knew I was going to be OK.

Throughout the wait, I kept thinking of the hot shower I would enjoy once I got to the French Quarter. And I felt like a half-drowned river rat as I carted my rain-drenched belongings past the concierges at the historic Place d'Armes Hotel in the heart of the Quarter. Members of a Chinese tour group stared at me with mouths agape, probably wondering what sort of a hotel they had been booked into. I mustered a smile and said to them through chattering teeth, "Ni *hao*" ("hello"). They all bowed.

A hot shower had never felt so good. I must have fallen asleep under the water jet and awoke about a half-hour later. Then it was time for dinner. It was a meal that I had looked forward to during my entire trip – for the previous four months and 22 days – a gathering of a select group of friends at a restaurant called Mothers.

Wynette Jameson is a veteran high school journalism teacher who had offered encouragement for my expedition from concept to completion. I was very touched that she had taken the day off work to drive from Houston. She was joined by one of her former star pupils, Chris Kirkham, who had shared in the 2006 Pulitzer Prize for Public Service, awarded to *The Times-Picayune* for its coverage of Hurricane Katrina. Wynette and Chris were fans of Dan Eldon, and Wynette was a friend of Dan's mother, Kathy Eldon, the lady behind Dan's Facebook page. Wynette had introduced me to Kathy and put me in touch with the Creative Visions Foundation in Malibu, Calif., established by Kathy and her daughter, Amy, to honor Dan.

And here we all were, sharing a table with my Oxford-based friends, Bob and Jane Pekala, supping on crawfish *etouffee*, red beans and rice, jambalaya and po'boys, washing it all down with Dixie and Abita beer. It was a magical night. We laughed and drank, swapped stories and snapped photos. That night I replayed the journey in my mind, over and over, in slow motion. It was glorious.

The next morning, all of my friends were headed home, save for Chris, who lives in New Orleans. We met again the next night to talk about a Katrina-related story I hoped to do. I told Chris I was interested in Brad Pitt's nonprofit organization Make It Right NOLA. He said that the Katrina story had been approached from every possible angle, except maybe for one: that residents of the devastated Lower Ninth Ward were rebuilding in concert with a newfound love of environmentalism. He gave me contact information for Make It Right NOLA and said to tell the staff that he had recommended me.

Tom Darden, 30, was executive director of the organization, and I talked with him in front of a series of enlarged photographs of the Lower Ninth Ward, showing the neighborhood before and after Katrina and the rebuilding under way.

"Make It Right was founded by Brad Pitt after Hurricane Katrina, about two years after the storm," Darden said. "The community was still totally devastated. And so our mission is to build green, affordable, safe, healthy homes for families of the Lower Ninth Ward who want to rebuild their community. I think the fact that nonprofits, that individuals, volunteers from all over the world came to New Orleans after the storm really points to the absence of government's response.

"Neighborhoods like the Lower Ninth Ward have just been inundated with experts from all over the world. Our architects are great examples of that. We've got 21 different architectural firms, some from the city of New Orleans, but some from as far away as Tokyo, Japan, or Ghana, Africa … I think that really says a lot, not just about the families who are from the Lower Ninth Ward who are really pioneers in coming home and rebuilding, but also about the volunteers and about the nonprofits from all over who have dedicated their time and their resources to come down and help."

Thanks to Katrina, the Lower Ninth Ward is one of the best known neighborhoods in America, and it is now undergoing a transformation from the poster child of hurricane destruction into a national example of green, sustainable living.

Dr. Douglas Meffert of Tulane University's Center for Bioenvironmental Research picked me up and we drove to the part of the Lower Ninth Ward adjacent to the breach in the levee wall where the Mississippi River came crashing through. Here, the neighborhood was mostly vacant lots. The only evidence that homes once stood here were brick steps and cement foundation slabs. A tall white egret walked past the car with its deliberate, funny-legged gait and then lifted off, flying just outside the driver-side window. "That's an ecosystem service – wildlife," he said. "There's a wetland habitat reclaiming itself. That is part of what the Lower Ninth Ward is."

We drove to the other side of the Lower Ninth Ward, where concern for the environment is playing a big role in the rebuilding.

"We're here at Bayou Bienvenue," Professor Meffert said with a sweep of his tweed-jacketed arm. "If you went back 80 years, you would have seen a thriving cypress-tupelo swamp." A few green sprouts were pushing up from the murk, and this, I was told, is a good sign. He said that the plantings were the work of Make it Right and students from the University of Wisconsin.

"It's going back to the way we looked at water as an advantage, not just something to be taken for granted like the Mississippi River, or something to be seen as a threat in terms of storm surge and flooding," he said. "So on this end they're looking back to the bayou to restore it and to provide amenities and ecological services for the community. And then when you go towards the Mississippi River, on the other end, above sea level, we're even exploring the possibility of generating renewable energy. So for me, this is a perfect example of living with water in a way that not only sustains but benefits the community in the long term."

Later, I walked around the Lower Ninth Ward on my own. Along the levee I saw where a barge had pushed through the breach. Some utility poles still leaned at odd angles; others had been replaced or righted. Brad Pitt and former President Bill Clinton had recently broken ground for new houses in the neighborhood, to be occupied by returning residents. A throng of builders in hard hats had been on hand at the groundbreaking, shovels, hammers and other tools at the ready. Here stood the result of their labor, 15 completed Make it Right homes, with more under construction. The homes had a modern look, some painted bright colors and some with solar panels on the roofs.

I paused on Tennessee Street to read a sign that said: "I AM COMING HOME – I WILL REBUILD! – I AM NEW ORLEANS." Someone had covered the word "COMING" with duct tape. I photographed the sign and a group of wreaths laid to honor those who had died near the spot. As I was taking pictures, the occupant of a new house came out with a smile and an outstretched hand. I told him I was working on a story about rebuilding in the Lower Ninth Ward. "That's me. I'm living that story," he said.

The man was Robert Lynn Green Sr., a retired tax accountant. He was a giant of a man, wearing a New Orleans Saints jersey. He showed me a memorial marker next to his new home, explaining that he'd lost his grandmother and granddaughter to Katrina. "Til the end of time, We miss and love you both," said the gray granite stone, which had a small collection of smooth river stones just above the names. The grandmother, Joyce, was born in 1931. The granddaughter,

Shanai, had been only 3. The date of death for both was Aug. 29, 2005.

This present flood of 1882 will doubtless be celebrated in the river's history for several generations before a deluge of like magnitude shall be seen. It put all the unprotected low lands under water, from Cairo to the mouth; it broke down the levees in a great many places, on both sides of the river; and in some regions south, when the flood was at its highest, the Mississippi was seventy miles wide! A number of lives were lost, and the destruction of property was fearful. The crops were destroyed, houses washed away, and shelterless men and cattle forced to take refuge on scattering elevations here and there in field and forest, and wait in peril and suffering until the boats put in commission by the national and local governments and by newspaper enterprise could come and rescue them. The properties of multitudes of people were under water for months, and the poorer ones must have starved by the hundred if succor had not been promptly afforded.

—*Life on the Mississippi*, 1883, Chapter 26

We stood on a set of front steps, all that remained of Green's old house – the empty lot now in the shadow of the new home next-door. He invited me in for coffee and a chat. As we climbed the steps, I asked how he felt about the move.

"This is the same neighborhood where I played football in the streets as a kid, where my kids played football in the streets, where me and my granddaughters used to walk every day and say hello to our neighbors," he said, gesturing toward the street. "What this new home means to us is – we're back home. My grandkids come, my children come – kids who lived here before. It's our way of regaining what we had before Katrina. So this is basically where we are rebuilding our lives and starting new in a greener and better way. Come on inside and see the house."

Green was clearly proud of his new home, elevated on stilts to keep the living space above any future floods. As we did a quick tour, he showed off family photographs and spoke of the house's energy-saving features. "You know, it's funny," he said. "I've become an environmentalist living in this house."

Over coffee, we talked of the hurricane that had changed his life, took the lives of his mother and granddaughter and killed at least 1,800 other people in New Orleans and along the Gulf Coast.

"The morning of Katrina, at 4 o'clock in the morning," he began, "my brother Jonathan woke us up to say, 'Robert, we have water in the house.' We had five minutes to get from downstairs into the attic. And when we got into the attic, we thought we were safe because we were higher up. He kicked the vent out and looked outside and said, 'Robert, this is not going to work, we gotta get to the roof.' So we began kicking at the ceiling in the attic with our feet and made a hole so we could climb out the attic, and while we were climbing out the attic the water was continuing to rise. And basically our house started to float. When the house on the left hit it and the house on the right hit it, it began floating down the street.

"So, Katrina for us was a pretty bad experience because my granddaughter died at 4:30 in the morning, and my mother died at 1 o'clock the next day. So we lost two family members on that day. We lost all of our neighbors. We were floating past everybody's house – past Mr. Gaskin's house, past Mr. Leggett's house, past Mrs. Gloria's house, past Ms. Guy's house, past Irene. We were just floating past all my neighbors. And while we were on the roof of the house, where we are sitting right now was actually under water. So, basically, it was a pretty bad hurricane."

A couple blocks down the street, at a white clapboard church, I met Darryl Malek-Wiley, regional representative and environmental justice organizer for the Sierra Club. The church, like others in the Lower Ninth Ward, had become an unofficial community center, where neighbors met and where essential goods were distributed to people most in need.

Malek-Wiley was waiting on the street. He sported a white linen suit that matched his white hair and long beard. We went into the church and sat in a pew to talk.

"What we're seeing with the Make It Right project and other projects here in the Lower Ninth Ward is a series of projects driven by the community understanding their close connection with the environment," Malek-Wiley said. "It's driven by a sense of, 'If we can make our houses better, we don't have to pay as high an energy bill.'

"Understanding sustainability is not a new thing," he continued. "The historic homes that were built in this neighborhood were sustainable for the time. They were built out of renewable resources – wood. They were built to take advantage of the natural breezes. They had lots of cross ventilation, they had high ceilings to keep the heat away. So sustainability is not a new buzzword – they did it here in the 1860s, '70s, '80s and '90s. What we're doing now is taking the newer green technologies and retrofitting them on a number of those houses."

Recalling my stop at Bayou Bienvenue with Dr. Meffert, I asked how reestablishment of the once-thriving cypress-tupelo swamp tied in with the green rebuilding effort.

"Yes, yes," Malek-Wiley said, eager to explain. "One of the things I think is key about the Lower Ninth Ward and their vision of sustainability – it's not just green rebuilding of houses or new houses, it's about rebuilding the natural protection of the Louisiana coast – our big cypress forest, our wetlands, our coast. It doesn't matter if we're building the greenest houses in the world, if we're not restoring our natural coast, it's not going to matter."

Aside from the natural protection against flooding afforded by wetlands, I asked, what other uses would Bayou Bienvenue have?

"Historically, folks in the neighborhood would go out

there and hunt, fish, recreate," Malek-Wiley said. "Kids would go out there to get away from their parents, all the things kids love to do. But then the Corps of Engineers built the Mississippi River Gulf Outlet in 1965, and it allowed salt water to come in and kill all the cypress trees. So, not only the cypress trees in the Bienvenue area, right there at the Lower Ninth Ward, but almost 30,000 acres of coastal wetland cypress were killed. So the neighborhood has been looking at, how do we restore, how do we rebuild the whole 30,000 back into coastal wetland and swamp – cypress trees – because if we don't have those natural protections, levees are not enough."

From the Lower Ninth Ward, I went back to the French Quarter, and then walked through the Central Business District and along the oak-lined streets of the Garden District, headed for Tulane University. There I wanted to sum up what I had learned with Professor Marc Davis, director of the Tulane Institute on Water Resources Law and Policy.

I asked him about media stories questioning the wisdom of rebuilding in New Orleans, large portions of which are below sea level and prone to frequent flooding. This was a topic of considerable debate in this old, proud city, as many New Orleanians felt that the nation was ready to write them off.

"All coasts are floodplains and river cities tend to be in floodplains – and they're there *for a reason*," the professor began, warming to a topic that he obviously had thought deeply about. "So the issue is not, 'Is it crazy to live here?' It's under what terms and conditions can we and should we. It's built on an honest respect that we don't understand all the forces, or all the values.

"Nature always bats last, so we need to be, I think, far more respectful of the power of nature and our ability to control it. We can push it around, as though the wetlands have no value. And now we know they're closer to being priceless. After all, New Orleans is here because of a relationship between the river, the continent and the oceans of the world. A city had to be here, however difficult it would be. And it's the reason that Jefferson bought not only New Orleans, but the Louisiana Purchase. They knew that the rest of it meant nothing without a city where New Orleans is. I think that by being respectful of not only our nature, but our history, we make better choices for the future."

His closing words seemed to say it all. They summed up what I had learned all along the Mississippi, from Lake Itasca to New Orleans. In its foulest of moods, this mighty river can deal death and destruction, as in the great floods of 1882, 1927 and 1993. But it is also a source of great bounty – an irrigator of crops, a treasure house of aquatic food, a magnet for waterfowl and other wild game, a natural trade corridor whose tributaries reach into 31 states, and an outlet for the produce of a nation. Like other great rivers, however, the Mississippi resists the hand of man and demands respect. As Mark Twain wrote of the Mississippi: "It cannot be tamed, curbed or confined. ... You cannot bar its path with an obstruction which it will not tear down, dance over and laugh at. The Mississippi will always have its own way, no engineering skill can persuade it to do otherwise."

I shook hands with the professor and took my leave. The story now seemed complete. I caught the St. Charles streetcar and headed back to the French Quarter. Feeling surprisingly empty and alone, I phoned Chris Kirkham at the *Times-Picayune* to see if he might be up for a drink.

Over healthy doses of restorative bourbon, Chris volunteered to help me shoot a final report for CNN. Using my camera, Chris framed a shot of me – with scraggly beard, sunburned nose and a look of disreputable bedraggledness. He used as a backdrop the Greater New Orleans Bridge and the riverside boardwalk, just as the sun was setting. This, fittingly, would be the "sunset" report of my adventure on the river.

Now when I had mastered the language of this water and had come to know every trifling feature that bordered the great river as familiarly as I knew the letters of the alphabet, I had made a valuable acquisition. But I had lost something, too. I had lost something which could never be restored to me while I lived. All the grace, the beauty, the poetry had gone out of the majestic river! I still keep in mind a certain wonderful sunset which

I witnessed when steamboating was new to me. A broad expanse of the river was turned to blood; in the middle distance the red hue brightened into gold, through which a solitary log came floating, black and conspicuous; in one place a long, slanting mark lay sparkling upon the water; in another the surface was broken by boiling, tumbling rings, that were as many-tinted as an opal; where the ruddy flush was faintest, was a smooth spot that was covered with graceful circles and radiating lines, ever so delicately traced; the shore on our left was densely wooded, and the somber shadow that fell from this forest was broken in one place by a long, ruffled trail that shone like silver; and high above the forest wall a clean-stemmed dead tree waved a single leafy bough that glowed like a flame in the unobstructed splendor that was flowing from the sun. There were graceful curves, reflected images, woody heights, soft distances; and over the whole scene, far and near, the dissolving lights drifted steadily, enriching it, every passing moment, with new marvels of coloring.

I stood like one bewitched. I drank it in, in a speechless rapture. The world was new to me, and I had never seen anything like this at home. But as I have said, a day came when I began to cease from noting the glories and the charms which the moon and the sun and the twilight wrought upon the river's face; another day came when I ceased altogether to note them. Then, if that sunset scene had been repeated, I should have looked upon it without rapture, and should have commented upon it, inwardly, after this fashion: This sun means that we are going to have wind to-morrow; that floating log means that the river is rising, small thanks to it; that slanting mark on the water refers to a bluff reef which is going to kill somebody's steamboat one of these nights, if it keeps on stretching out like that; those tumbling 'boils' show a dissolving bar and a changing channel there; the lines and circles in the slick water over yonder are a warning that that troublesome place is shoaling up dangerously; that silver streak in the shadow of the forest is the 'break' from a new snag, and he has located himself in the very best place he could have found to fish for steamboats; that tall dead tree, with a single living branch, is not going to last long, and then how is a body ever going to get through this blind place at night without the friendly old landmark. No, the romance and the beauty were all gone from the river. All the value any feature of it had for me now was the amount of usefulness it could furnish toward compassing the safe piloting of a steamboat.

—*Life on the Mississippi*, 1883, Chapter 9

As if on cue, the paddle steamer Natchez tooted its whistle to announce its landing at the boardwalk to pick up a new load of tourists. I looked toward the steamboat and the river, to the postcard-perfect sunset, to the gulls wheeling over the boardwalk, and experienced one of those end-of-life moments. My entire expedition came back to me, rapid fire, in flashes – from launch to completion – a millisecond for each of the faces I'd encountered along the way.

"You're at the southern terminus of the Mississippi River –

New Orleans. It's been more than four months," Chris said into the microphone. "Tell us what you learned and take us back to the beginning, and tell us: Why the Mississippi River, and why this part of America?"

My brain was aswirl with thoughts of the journey – the people I met, the dangers I faced, the pure joy of drifting down the Mississippi like Huckleberry Finn. What to say? How to sum it up? I looked at Chris, at the camera and experienced a combination of elation, exhaustion and sheer satisfaction. At first, all I could do was smile.

AFTERWORD

CINDY LOVELL

"... and so there ain't nothing more to write about, and I am rotten glad of it, because if I'd a knowed what a trouble it was to make a book I wouldn't a tackled it, and ain't a-going to no more."

SO SAID HUCKLEBERRY FINN in the closing lines of Twain's masterpiece. Still, Huck went on to voice *Tom Sawyer Abroad* (1894) and *Tom Sawyer, Detective* (1896). So much for "ain't a-going to no more."

When Neal and I got to the end of our book I felt no such absolutes. I only felt that bittersweet pang that comes at journey's end – when you've arrived home and are glad to be there and the suitcases contain only dirty laundry and a few souvenirs. Final details await – uploading vacation pics to Facebook, resuming mail delivery, returning to the comfortable routine of job – but the trip is done.

Although I didn't meet Neal until roughly the halfway mark of his journey, our common bonds made it feel as though we'd always known each other. Our shared enthusiasm made us family. Tagging along from that point on – figuratively, as I remained in Hannibal only *wishing* to help paddle and, literally, by way of visits to St. Louis, Oxford and New Orleans – made jumping aboard the literary journey feel natural. Yes. We should write a book.

Neal was doing what every self-respecting Twainiac wishes to do. He was *in* The River. And on it. And alongside. He was in bright sun *and* harm's way. (Both sound appealing to the gentle reader paddling from an armchair.) Neal was attracting characters as they attracted him, and their stories poured forth. With every phone call, email, blog post and iReport came a celebration of the human condition's most intimate stories. We were all characters. We were all complicit. We were all cheering.

Sam Clemens, the steamboatman and itinerant journalist, enjoyed a fascination with the whole wide world. Clemens possessed an immense curiosity. He needed to know everything. Details were his nourishment, boredom an impossibility. Neal's notion of paddling Twain's river to collect and share positive stories about the people he encountered resonated with my inner-Huckleberry. A book. Yes, there must be a book. And Twain would certainly have something to say.

The plan couldn't be simpler. Neal would do all the work – canoeing, surviving, reporting, celebrating – and I would cheer him on. Then, at journey's end, we'd write a book. And so we have. And now both journeys have ended – Neal's waterway adventure, and our shared encounter with words and paragraphs and pages and the wish to make tangible the voiced hopes Neal heard along the way.

Mark Twain jotted notes on the pages of books as he read. He generally reserved his marginalia for passages he loved or those he loathed. As I read Neal's narrative, I listened for Twain to chime in on "that now-departed and hardly-remembered raft-life…"

> *"In the heyday of the steamboating prosperity, the river from end to end was flaked with coal-fleets and timber rafts, all managed by hand, and employing hosts of the rough characters whom I have been trying to describe. I remember the annual processions of mighty rafts that used to glide by Hannibal when I was a boy, – an acre or so of white, sweet-smelling boards in each raft, a crew of two dozen men or more, three or four wigwams scattered about the raft's vast level space for storm-quarters, – and I remember the rude ways and the tremendous talk of their big crews, the ex-keelboatmen… for we used to swim out a quarter or third of a mile and get on these rafts and have a ride."*

—*Life on the Mississippi*, 1883, Chapter 3

Thank you, Neal, for letting me swim out and ride along.

—Cindy Lovell, Hannibal, 2012

ACKNOWLEDGEMENTS

NEAL MOORE

I'D LIKE TO THANK MY FRIEND and mentor, the late Basil Nott, as well as the life-as-a-safari examples of Dan Eldon and a representative of the next generation of adventure-activist-filmmakers, Liam Erasmus. Thanks to Jim Peipert, Ralph Hinkson, Louis Stephany, Lew and Maureen Moore, Kathy Eldon and Wynette Jameson, who encouraged me on this expedition from planning through completion; my agent, Ken Wright at Writers House, who has valiantly represented this book; Jim Peipert again for his diligent editing of both the written word and photographic work contained herein;

Emily Larson Hayes, Danny Wilson and Kurt Multhaup for their proofing; Bob and Jane Pekala for their love and belief in this story; Amy Wilson and Mark Stocker for their friendship and direction; Zarina Rose Lagman for stepping in on short notice to design the book's cover and interior; Arron Hsueh at DDG for his canoeist logo and Mississippi River map; Tope Sosanya for his web design; and the many hamlets, towns and cities nestled along the banks of the Mighty Mississippi that opened their doors and their hearts and trusted me to share their stories.

Thanks to my producer, Henry Hanks, at CNN and the entire Team iReport and CNN.com; Kathleen Parkarinen of the *Independent Age* of Aitkin, Minn.; Dan Moris of PdCToday.com of Prairie du Chien, Wis.; Danny Henley of the *Hannibal Courier-Post*; Ed Husar and Rodney Hart of the *Quincy Herald-Whig*; Big River magazine; CBS affiliate KHQA-TV; NBC affiliate WGEM-TV; Nicholas Phillips of the *Daily RFP*; Jon Scott and Alyssa Schnugg of *The Oxford Eagle*; Joseph Williams of *The Oxford Enterprise*; Craig Guillot of PackandExplore.com; and Jim Peipert of Jim's Bike Blog for their reports on the journey. Also a great debt of thanks for my whirlwind tour of CNN Center, specifically for the chance to meet and discuss these stories with Andreas Preuss, Victor Hernandez and Nancy Lane, who kindly took time out of their busy schedules to share their insight and encouragement.

Special thanks to my co-author and friend, Cindy Lovell, for her friendship, for conjuring Mark Twain, and for her camaraderie in planning the stories in this book, along with her entire staff at the Mark Twain Boyhood Home & Museum: Henry Sweets, Ryan Murray, Dena Whitaker Ellis and Mai Conrad, for entrusting to me the key for my night in Sam Clemens' bedroom. Thanks to those mentioned in this book who provided a couch, bed or patch of grass on which to pitch my tent, along with: Donald Keith Butler, Ron Florio of Florio's Grill and Tavern, Daryl Ledger, the brothers Wallenfang, John Dodegge, the Keokuk Yacht Club, Deb Hopper, Tug Buce, George and Marcia Wessitsh, the Rev. Chan Osborn de Anaya, Adam Elliott, Michael Beck, Sandrea Everett and Virginia Miller.

I'd also like to thank the many greasy-spoon eateries where I sought shelter, contacts, electricity, story backdrops, key lime pie and a good healthy dose of Americana, without which this book would not have been possible: Trails End Restaurant, Blackduck, Minn.; Palisade Café, Palisade, Minn.; Birchwood Café, Aitkin, Minn.; West Side Café, Little Falls, Minn.; Wilde Roast Café, Minneapolis, Minn.; Maggie's Diner, McGregor, Iowa; Thoma Dairy Bar Cafe, Garnavillo, Iowa; Grandpa John's Café, Nauvoo, Ill.; Java Jive and the Mark Twain Dinette, Hannibal, Mo.; The Nu Diner, Cairo, Ill.; Delta Amusement Café, Clarksdale, Miss.; The Bottletree Bakery and the Ajax Diner, Oxford, Miss.; and the Clover Grill, New Orleans, La.

AND TO THE ORGANIZATIONS FEATURED IN THIS BOOK, THANK YOU!

The Leech Lake Band of Ojibwe, Relay for Life, Creative Visions Foundation, The Brian Coyle Center, ArtiCulture, Minnesota International Middle School, Practical Farmers of Iowa, Mark Twain Boyhood Home & Museum, Habitat for Humanity St. Louis, Youth Villages, Volunteer MidSouth, The Blues Foundation, Quapaw Canoe Co., Cat Head Delta Blues & Folk Art, Square Books, Thacker Mountain Radio, Lafayette County Literacy Council, The Powerhouse, University of Mississippi Museum, KIPP Charter School of Helena, Ark., Louisiana State Penitentiary at Angola and Make It Right NOLA.

—Neal Moore, 2012

Cindy Lovell is a Huck Finn-inspired high school dropout with a Ph.D. A "Twainiac" since age 10, she has serendipitously found herself serving as executive director of the Mark Twain Boyhood Home & Museum in Hannibal, Mo. She also serves as an associate professor of education at Quincy University in Quincy, Ill. When it comes to "talking Twain," her ex-husband said it best: "Don't get her started!"

Neal Moore is a world traveler, creative activist and international citizen journalist whose reporting has taken him from night-market meetings with Chinese cyber-dissidents to mountaintop encounters with approaching super typhoons. His dispatches from North America and the Far East have appeared on Headline News, "Anderson Cooper 360°" and CNN International. He lives in Cape Town, South Africa.

CPSIA information can be obtained at www.ICGtesting.com
Printed in the USA
LVOW131709260912

300442LV00016B/2/P

9 780983 716921